MALLED

MALLED

MY UNINTENTIONAL CAREER IN RETAIL

CAITLIN KELLY

PORTFOLIO / PENGUIN

PORTFOLIO / PENGUIN
Published by the Penguin Group
Penguin Group (USA) Inc., 375 Hudson Street, New York, New York 10014, U.S.A.
Penguin Group (Canada), 90 Eglinton Avenue East, Suite 700, Toronto, Ontario, Canada M4P 2Y3
(a division of Pearson Penguin Canada Inc.)
Penguin Books Ltd, 80 Strand, London WC2R 0RL, England
Penguin Ireland, 25 St. Stephen's Green, Dublin 2, Ireland
(a division of Penguin Books Ltd)
Penguin Books Australia Ltd, 250 Camberwell Road, Camberwell, Victoria 3124, Australia
(a division of Pearson Australia Group Pty Ltd)
Penguin Books India Pvt Ltd, 11 Community Centre, Panchsheel Park, New Delhi – 110 017, India
Penguin Group (NZ), 67 Apollo Drive, Rosedale, North Shore 0632, New Zealand
(a division of Pearson New Zealand Ltd)
Penguin Books (South Africa) (Pty) Ltd, 24 Sturdee Avenue Rosebank, Johannesburg 2196, South Africa

Penguin Books Ltd, Registered Offices: 80 Strand, London WC2R 0RL, England

First published in 2011 by Portfolio / Penguin, a member of Penguin Group (USA) Inc.

1   3   5   7   9   10   8   6   4   2

LIBRARY OF CONGRESS CATALOGING IN PUBLICATION DATA
Kelly, Caitlin.
Malled : my unintentional career in retail / Caitlin Kelly.
p.   cm.
ISBN 978-1-59184-380-1
1. Selling   2. Selling—Vocational guidance.   3. Retail trade.   I. Title.
HF5438.25.K447 2011
658.85—dc22   2010043590

Printed in the United States of America
Set in Adobe Jenson
Designed by Spring Hoteling

Penguin is committed to publishing works of quality and integrity. In that spirit, we are proud to offer this book to our readers; however, the story, the experiences, and the words are the author's alone.

To all those who serve the public—
especially those who do it with skill and pleasure

CONTENTS

CONTENTS

AUTHOR'S NOTE

This book is a recollection of the two years and three months I worked as a retail sales associate for The North Face, with additional reporting and research completed after I formally gave two weeks' notice and left the company. Neither the company nor my coworkers knew I was writing it; I have changed all their names. Whatever errors or omissions occur are mine; I took copious notes for several months but have also written from memory, and some events appear out of chronological order. Every character is a real person I worked with and none are composites.

Unless otherwise noted, and cited as a secondary source, all the interviews in this book are original and were conducted directly with the interview subjects by me or my research assistants by telephone, in person, or by e-mail.

My interviews with other retail workers outside the company, with their permission, retain their true identities; only Sarah McFarlane is a pseudonym. I've also used pseudonyms for some *Daily News* staff.

MALLED

INTRODUCTION

You're probably going to buy something today—gas, groceries, a double-skim latte, diapers, a pack of gum, or maybe a dress or a pair of sneakers. You'll swipe your credit or debit card, or pay cash, or maybe write a check and hand it to someone standing in front of you, since we still make 90 percent of our purchases in person.

But who is that person standing across from you? Do you ever stop to think about it?

What if it were you standing behind that counter, wearing that plastic badge, your sweaty feet aching, desperate for a pee or a cold drink, counting the minutes until your break? (If you even get one.)

For two years and three months—rare in an industry with 100 percent turnover every year—that person was me. I worked for The North Face, an internationally known brand of outdoor clothing and equipment, selling merchandise in a company store in a suburban mall. From its opening in October 2007 until I left in December 2009, we were consistently among their top five bestselling stores (of sixteen, then thirty nationwide), often among the top three. With fourteen other full- and part-time coworkers, I sold shoes and sleeping bags and backpacks, jackets made of nylon and fleece, thick ski gloves and cotton caps and T-shirts to teachers and tourists, psychologists and athletes, surgeons and hedge-fund managers. I had never before worked retail, except for a brief teenage stint in a small Toronto drugstore where I handled the cash register and sullenly refilled shelves.

Instead, I'd spent my life as a shopper, an author, a reporter, a world traveler, a wife.

Moving to the other side of the cash wrap—that's what they call the counter where the cash registers are, where you complete your purchase—felt as disorienting to me as Alice might have felt when she slipped through the mirror into Wonderland, landing unawares in an unfamiliar world populated by Mad Hatters, rushing rabbits, chatty chess pieces, and enormous mushrooms. By moving to the other side of the register, I, too, entered a new world, one I had only glimpsed in passing since I was little.

I still remember some of the first things I ever bought with my allowance or Christmas or birthday money, like a black marble egg and an antique silver egg cup I bought in a store in Edinburgh when I was twelve, and gave to my Mom. Shopping was a special activity then.

Now everyone shops. It's a sport, a game, and an amusing and social way to kill time. But not in our family, and certainly not back in the 1960s and 1970s when I was growing up in Toronto. Then, I shopped rarely, and usually with my exotic, imperious, multiply divorced American grandmother Aline, a grande dame in raw-silk, custom-made muumuus and matching turbans topped with huge, real jewels. Granny doted on me, her only grandchild.

Shopping with Granny was a trip. She was the sort of customer that, years later as an associate myself, I would come to loathe: demanding, fussy, rich, prone to tantrums if the service failed to meet her stratospheric expectations. I can still remember, at the age of nine or ten, wanting to disappear through the floor at Holt Renfrew, Canada's 174-year-old high-end department store chain, as she pitched yet another fit over whatever had just displeased her.

INTRODUCTION

I *did* love receiving her Holt's gifts at Christmas, in those days distinctively wrapped in thick silver paper tied with cobalt-blue ribbon. I could spot a Holt's box from across the room and, like other lucky Canadians, knew it would always contain something lovely.

It never occurred to me that I'd one day be standing behind a counter myself.

My writing career had gone well from the day I graduated from college, whether I had a staff magazine or newspaper job or worked freelance. But by the fall of 2007 I was scared of the precipitous decline in my industry, journalism. I was also newly aware, after pneumonia landed me in a hospital bed from overwork, I needed a ready, steady source of cash, *something* solid.

And so I decided to join a populous, if largely ignored, tribe—the fifteen million Americans working in retail, one million of whom sell apparel.

We all have to sell ourselves, to get or keep a job or win a promotion, grant, or fellowship. Even a first date, if you like the person and hope for another meeting, is a sales job. I figured selling skills, if it turned out I even *had* any, could only be helpful in the future, no matter what I did professionally. I'd always found it difficult reaching out to new clients—who likes rejection?

The North Face sells its products worldwide through hundreds of other retailers in addition to their own freestanding stores. I knew and liked their stuff. Living in New York, at least, you see their products everywhere, from the backpacks lugged by middle-aged male commuters jamming the train into Manhattan from Connecticut or Long Island, to the wildly popular fleece and nylon jackets worn by their teenage kids, desperate for that coveted curved logo. Their products looked decent. I figured they couldn't be that difficult to sell, since so many people already knew and loved the brand.

But putting on a white plastic badge with my name carved into it proved a powerful eye-opener in many ways. I had never worked in any job that paid so little for such hard work. The American economy relies heavily on consumer spending—70 percent of its GDP. Yet retail sales associates, clerks, floorwalkers, team members—whatever you choose call them—remain oddly invisible in the media, even as we buy from them every day. Their lives, their needs, and their concerns, whether for safe, clean workplaces or livable wages, often go ignored, both by reporters more attentive to corporate profit projections and by the many corporations who employ millions of associates and rely so heavily on them. Most workers doing these tough jobs for low wages are those least able to afford losing them. They have a powerful incentive to remain silent.

Rarely, then, do you hear what it's really like to do this ubiquitous job, one that's practically a rite of passage for many Americans. I wanted to know more, as a journalist, a shopper, and an avid daily reader of the business press. Virtually every retail story I read quoted only Wall Street retail analysts, when it's more often the frontline workers whose energy, patience, and skills—or lack of same—so profoundly affect how we, the consumers, perceive and value a company's product or service.

In 2009, three young female reporters, one each from *The New York Times*, *Fortune*, and *SmartMoney*, went to work as retail associates, only for a week or so. Each was shocked at how hard this work is. Anyone who's put in time behind a register or rummaged through a dusty, dirty, disorganized stockroom learns quickly the gap between the shiny, brightly lit sales floor and the chaos behind the scenes.

And the median retail wage remains a crummy $8.92 per hour, even as *one-fifth of American business is retail*, worth $4 trillion a year. Thirty-four percent of employees work part-time, many of them with no job-related benefits.

We all shop, all the time, even if only for the barest necessities: food, medicine, toilet paper. Women make up 80 percent of shoppers, exerting tremendous influence. We deal firsthand, then, almost daily with a huge army of associates, workers earning persistently low wages at the tail end of a costly, complex global supply chain whose every twist and turn, including design, marketing, branding, and advertising, is chronicled by the press. Sales are consistently and zealously pumped by enormous expenditures on everything from mirrors that record a shopper's gender, age, and height to hiring a classical pianist, as Apple did in January 2010 when Leif Ove Andsnes played Janáček and Mussorgsky in their new Upper West Side location.

Yet in the great arms race to keep the American shopper spending, whether a tween snagging some leggings at Delia's or a seventy-five-year-old picking up Lipitor at CVS, the sales associate remains the most overlooked and least valued piece of the equation.

We still make 85 percent of our buying decisions only after arriving in the store. A lousy or lazy clerk can send you spinning right back onto the street, frustrated, empty-handed, and indignant—or a good one can help you happily spend all sorts of money on items you hadn't planned to purchase that day, maybe ever.

While retail associates remain the grunts of our consumption-based economy, they also, paradoxically, retain tremendous power. We've all been through it. One rude or indifferent interaction with an associate can sabotage the sexiest million-dollar ad campaign; an annoyed customer typically warns at least ten others away from a company's service or product. Add the powerful multiplier effect of social media and Web sites like targetsucks.blogspot.com, and even one lousy experience can, and does, easily go viral. Associates, and their managers, can and do every single day destroy shoppers' elusive and fickle desire to buy carefully burnished brands—or initiate and foster customer gratitude, loyalty, return business, and huge profits for their employers. Yet, despite this arguably crucial role, associates typically receive little or no respect, whether from shoppers, their bosses, or those who study, write about, or otherwise profit from their labor and skills.

Very few people pay attention to associates.

In his bestseller *Why We Buy*, retail consultant Paco Underhill, CEO of the twenty-six-year-old Manhattan firm Envirosell, devotes only a few sentences to these crucial human links between company and consumer. "Most firms are constantly looking to save money on labor," he writes, and are dancing the razor's edge between cutting their costs by reducing staff hours, and thereby possibly upping shoppers' frustration, and confusion with poor, even nonexistent service. "Many retailers," he adds—without further commentary—"underpay and undervalue their sales staff."

Only by working a regular shift month after month, year after year, through holidays, back-to-school frenzies, Black Friday sales, and January returns, did I start to understand retail. And, unlike most associates, 50 percent of whom are gone within ninety days of being hired, I stayed, working part-time, for two years and three months, from September 25, 2007, to December 18, 2009.

I liked the job a lot when I started and for a long time couldn't picture myself quitting. I liked having a set routine, a good-looking, comfortable, free company-supplied uniform, and a break from my work as a writer. I loved learning and perfecting new skills. I really enjoyed the variety of our customers and my friendly coworkers. I liked learning about the products, some of them fairly bristling with technical details, and selling them well. I appreciated being part of a small team within an international company whose products are well known and liked.

It took years for my early enthusiasm to wane, but it did. By the time I quit, giving two weeks' notice and choosing the quietest time of the year, when associates' hours are typically reduced in January anyway to save on labor costs, I knew they wouldn't need me and no longer cared if they might miss me personally or professionally. My initial zeal was long gone. And by then I was running on fumes. Nothing could have persuaded me to stay. My early pleasure in the work and the products and the company couldn't be regained or refreshed. Completely burned out, I only wanted to flee. The money was too low, our clients too spoiled and demanding, the work unceasingly dull and repetitive.

Those hiring retail associates enjoy ready access to a huge pool of workers, many of them, like me, experienced professionals, some even these days seeking a new career. But few associates, equally embittered and burned out by corporate gamesmanship, low pay, and dull, hard work, will ever stay long enough to gain any new skills or move up internally. Something is very wrong indeed when thousands of workers, every year, simply cycle through these jobs so quickly, many vowing never to return. Some, surely, are indeed ill-suited to the work or have been fired or move on to other ambitions. But those of us who like it and are good at it need to see a sea change in how this brutal business is often run.

Customers deserve, and want, much better. Healthy profits reward the few retailers who hire carefully, manage thoughtfully, train well and consistently, and pay associates well—and productive ones even better—and link managers' compensation to employee retention, as exemplars like Trader Joe's, Costco, The Container Store, and others have learned. As these companies know, retailing can be enjoyable and rewarding for shoppers and associates alike.

Come. Step behind the cash wrap for a while.

ONE

I SEEK REFUGE, AT THE MALL

It was time for a change. A big one.

A freelance writer with an unsteady and insecure income, despite years writing for markets like *The New York Times*, *The Wall Street Journal*, and *Glamour*, I was weary of chasing checks and haggling over payment. The industry, which hasn't raised its rates in thirty years because so many people are so eager to write, often without payment, had lost its allure.

I needed a new challenge.

After years of working at home alone, I was also lonely and isolated in a suburban New York apartment, without the distraction of kids or a pet, staring north up the Hudson River at the not-terribly-reassuring steam rising from a nuclear power plant.

I lived with my fiancé, Jose, a fellow career journalist, and had shared a life and home with him since 2001; his official moving day, when the trucks were loaded with his belongings to bring them from Brooklyn to my town, had been 9/11. We were both hardheaded world travelers, devotees of French bistros, news junkies. We met when I was reporting a magazine story on online dating and he replied to one of the listings I had placed for the assignment.

In 2007, I earned barely $20,000, less than a third of my best year's income. I wasn't earning enough because I'd begun to hate journalism. Not the writing; not the interviewing; not meeting and talking to everyone from convicted felons to Queen Elizabeth—I loved all of those aspects of journalism. I never tired of unpacking people's dreams and demons, no matter who they were, and translating them into stories. But, after more than a decade of freelancing, I was fed up with the growing gap between its putative freedom and the constant hustle.

And while I loved watching red-tailed hawks soar past my windows and rainstorms sliding across the river like a scrim, I just couldn't face another year of all-day solitude. I wanted to try something new, but craved (did this exist?) something simple and steady. Something that would pay me promptly and regularly. I needed gas and grocery money; my writing would cover, as it usually had for years, the big-ticket items like the mortgage and my retirement savings.

I needed a part-time job.

What I really needed most was a physical place outside my home where a boss and coworkers and a company would once more count on me. People might get to know me and like me, ask how my weekend went. We'd have in-jokes and a shared history.

But doing what?

I didn't want to pump gas or be a telemarketer or stock grocery shelves or slice meat in a deli or be a home health-care worker. I'd avoided learning marketable and lucrative skills like HTML, Photoshop, or Excel because I wanted work away from a computer. I didn't want to be a waitress again or a busboy. I'd done both as a college sophomore. I also rejected dog-walking, babysitting, and tutoring. Too much teenage competition.

I was starved for lively conversation, lots of laughter, and authority over something beyond my living room sofa.

Reading my local paper, I saw in September 2007 a help wanted ad for The North Face, a national chain of high-end outdoor wear. The company was opening a new store in an upscale mall nearby, filled with high-end names like Versace, Tiffany, and Neiman Marcus, in an affluent county near New York City.

I had traveled to thirty-seven countries, spoke fluent French and good Spanish, and participated in many sports, from ice-skating to squash. I loved sharing my passions for adventurous travel and the outdoors with others. It seemed like a good fit.

* * *

I'd been a journalist since my freshman year of college. It was all I'd ever wanted to be, and I'd gone on to work as a staff reporter and feature writer for three major dailies. I never had kids and never wanted them. My dream was to become a foreign correspondent filing features from Abidjan or Lima. My work had always given me more than a paycheck, offering adventures I never could have otherwise enjoyed, like flying through the middle of an iceberg on my way home from reporting a story in an Arctic village for the *Montreal Gazette*. A French truck driver ten years my senior took me on an eight-day journey from Perpignan to Istanbul. At twenty-three, I performed as an extra in the ballet *Sleeping Beauty* at Lincoln Center, sharing the stage with Rudolf Nureyev. I sipped a gin and tonic aboard the royal yacht *Britannia*, where I met Queen Elizabeth. I even spent five days aboard an Australian tall ship, scrambling a hundred feet up the rigging several times a day and sleeping in a tiny, swaying hammock every night.

It had been a year since I'd lost my job as a reporter and feature writer for the *New York Daily News*, the nation's sixth-largest newspaper. In July 2006, I was sliced out of my career with surgical speed at three p.m. on a Wednesday afternoon.

Colleagues had warned me that the only time I'd speak with Peter

McGillivray, a decades-entrenched senior manager at the *Daily News*, would be the day he fired me. It would, as it did, come in the form of an e-mail summons.

And there it was.

I walked into his dim, cramped office. Joe Campanelli, one of the men who had hired me, was reclining on the sofa, staring with disdain. My direct boss, Bill Harrison, was absent, struggling with a serious and ultimately fatal illness.

McGillivray, a pale, doughy guy who looked—like all senior managers there—like an outtake from the 1950s—leaned forward, his comb-over in place, a Kleenex box positioned nearby.

"We have to let you go," he said lugubriously.

I laughed. "Why?"

"Because you're not productive."

"You're kidding, right? Compared to who?"

In eleven months, I'd produced more than sixty stories; several were national scoops. Only two weeks earlier, I'd had "the wood," the paper's entire front page—a huge win every reporter competed for—with an exclusive piece about former New Jersey governor Jim McGreevey.

My tenure at the paper, my first-ever experience working full-time for a Manhattan daily or a tabloid, had been embattled from the start; I'd been hired by the paper's top editor, whom no one liked and who left within ten months. As someone who had freelanced for *The New York Times* since 1990, a bare-knuckled tabloid was a lousy fit for me, and my stories sat unused week after week while, frustrated, I watched the *Times*, *Time*, and *60 Minutes* jump on the same ideas sometimes long after mine were written and ready to go. But no *Daily News* editor would publish them.

I needed the income. Few people have the confidence or savings or a new job waiting to just walk out. I'd stayed and sucked it up.

That summer afternoon, I quietly said good-bye to half a dozen colleagues—several of whom appeared shocked and sad to see me go—and walked down the *News*'s long, narrow entrance hallway lined with enormous, iconic front pages of assassinations, executions, and elections. I would deeply miss being part of a major newspaper, scrambling all over the five boroughs on stories. I'd miss a few funny and kind colleagues.

* * *

I had no luck finding another job in journalism, at least one that paid more than I could make at home in sweatpants. I really missed being part of something—the excitement, the visibility, being relied upon, and knowing, and having other professionals appreciate, that I had something special to offer.

And it was increasingly difficult to watch my friends and fiancé—a photo editor for *The New York Times*—enjoy their work and be handsomely rewarded for it. I withdrew from my peers, my growing envy poisoning our few brief conversations.

At fifty, I was desperate to learn something new and, perhaps, become really good at it, while loath to assume graduate school debt to change careers without a clear direction.

Retail, like journalism, would push me into meeting dozens of strangers, something I knew how to do, liked, and was very good at. It would also offer, far from my own field, a clean slate and a risk-free fresh start. After my debacle at the *Daily News*, my self-confidence still battered, I needed a win. Few people I knew were likely to find me in a suburban mall store on a Tuesday afternoon. If I hated it, I could always just quit. It would never go on my résumé, and my odd little downscale pursuit would remain a secret shared only with close friends.

Still, taking an hourly retail job at the age of fifty, even if only for two days a week (which I quickly scaled back to one), felt like a giant and frightening step backward, the beginning of an inevitable slide down the socioeconomic ladder into the working class after decades of an upward climb in a profession I loved. I grew up attending private schools and summer camps, with a grandmother who went everywhere in a limousine, a father who won international awards for his documentary films, and a journalist mother whose glossy black mink had an emerald-green silk lining. My two younger half-brothers were doing well, one in policy work, the other running his own software company.

I charge $150 an hour for my writing and editorial skills—but knew I'd be lucky to get one-tenth of that in retail, a low-status job that most students were happy to leave after college. Was it even worth it?

Friends were supportive, if somewhat dubious. Why would I want to trade the comfort of working from home for an exhausting job on my feet all day? Wouldn't it be rough on my ego after seeing my by-lines in national magazines? Those who knew my short temper wondered if I'd even last a week.

And I'd spent very little time in sprawling suburban malls like the one that became my new workplace.

They represented everything I loathe: mass marketing, shoppers-as-sheep being herded efficiently from one overpriced stall to the next. Bad food, ugly carpeting, banal architecture, nasty music, TVs blaring ads overhead as you drag yourself with increasing weariness and dehydration up one side and down another, with only empty calories like oversized pretzels for mid-shopping sustenance. The national chains that populated malls seemed uncreative and soulless to me. Logos and brands left me cold.

And I had no retail experience. The last time I'd worked behind a counter was for a few months when I was seventeen in a Toronto drugstore, mostly blowing my tiny paycheck on the candy bars that lay within arm's reach. In the end, I figured if I could get jaded national magazine editors to buy my stories, surely I had *some* ability to sell things. I did know how to sell my own ideas to strangers and had been doing so since college.

Interviews for the new North Face store, like a hoofers' audition, were held at a local hotel, no appointment necessary. Accustomed only to more formal interviews in my field, I wasn't sure what to wear, and chose a simple Eileen Fisher black silk dress and plain black leather flats. I created a one-page résumé listing some of the skills I hoped might prove transferable, from worldwide travel and sports to cross-cultural fellowships. I admitted up-front, both verbally and in writing, that I had no retail experience.

The interview room was long and narrow, with rows of chairs mostly empty and two desks at the front occupied by two athletic-looking young men, one at each desk. Only three job-seekers were present when I arrived—a man in his fifties, maybe older, wearing a suit; a slim, curvaceous girl in her twenties, virtually poured into her orange jersey shirt-dress; and a sour-looking woman in her late fifties, maybe early sixties.

I was surprised to see so few applicants: the company was well known, its products widely counterfeited, and (in comparison to most newsrooms, which were crowded, cluttered, noisy bullpens) the mall was at least a clean, safe, dry, and warm work environment. Did no one want these jobs? Had everyone already come and gone? Was the money really that bad?

I could easily eavesdrop on the other three candidates, their interviews loud enough to be heard from the back of the room. The young girl yammered on for about twenty minutes, her ponytail bobbing and swinging, pouring on the charm.

The older man apologized for his thirty-year-old suit. Not a good sign. The older woman leaned on the interviewer's desk, and his eyes widened. She seemed stiff and angry, pushing hard for a job she maybe didn't really want but desperately needed.

"What do you think you can offer the company?" the interviewer finally asked, mildly. It was clear she had no satisfactory answer.

My turn.

It didn't feel like a job interview, but a long and congenial conversation. I was now alone in the room, no one else waiting impatiently behind me. The two managers, Joe Fields and Mike Knelman, were easygoing, smart, funny, relaxed white guys, who appeared to be in their thirties. We all talked for about half an hour. I liked them immediately and sensed they liked me. They didn't grill me or ask trick questions or demand I complete some stale personality test.

We just . . . talked.

Joe, with forearms as thick and powerful as thighs, had close-cropped graying hair, eyes the turquoise of a glacial lake, and a multicolored swirling tattoo running from his right wrist—encircled with a bone bead bracelet strung on leather—to his elbow. I'd never even met, let alone needed to impress, someone so inked. He didn't seem like some alienated punk, though. His manner was low-key, that of someone clearly comfortable with wielding authority, at ease in his own skin.

This laid-back, confident style was so unfamiliar that it was disorienting. I really liked it.

Almost every journalism job interview I'd had had been a sort of psychic dodgeball game, as I tried to guess, in the face of tough questions lobbed thick and fast, what they might find engaging, impressive, witty. I knew I could write but was terrible at selling myself. I had begun to dread, even avoid, job interviews as a result.

Joe and Mike were friendly and respectful. They didn't, as seemed to happen in every journalism interview, sneer at my work, laugh at my credentials, or dismiss decades of accomplishment. In their world, I'd actually done nothing—which somehow was just fine with them. (I later discovered this is pretty standard in retail, where many newcomers lack experience and are quickly brought up to speed.) Even clearly exhausted after a long day of interviews, the two didn't behave as though meeting me were an imposition, but seemed genuinely interested in what I might bring to the job.

The money, of course, was sobering, stunningly low. It was less than I had earned as a teenage lifeguard in the 1970s—$9 an hour for part-timers, $11 for full-time, with no commission or bonus, but with a healthy discount on company products. And I would have to pay $8 just to park in the mall's lot for my shift—in effect losing the first hour of my labor.

I asked for $11 an hour, working two days a week, Tuesdays from one to nine p.m. and Wednesdays during the day. That would still leave me three and a half days a week, if I didn't work weekends, for writing and editing assignments. I was a little nervous about giving up even a few hours of that time, but I'd really reached the end of my rope focusing all of my energy on one set of skills.

I walked out into the September sunshine. I had sent out forty-eight résumés applying for nonprofit communications or writing positions, a segue that many of my colleagues had repeatedly and enthusiastically assured me was a natural transition. I hadn't received a single reply.

Now, finally, I could feel it. I was about to be offered a job. I didn't care if it was retail. They liked me. They wanted me.

I was hired.

TWO
SETTLING IN

Our new team had fifteen members: twelve associates, a manager, and two assistant managers. We returned to the hotel once more, this time for four consecutive six-hour days of training.

I'd never *been* trained.

In journalism, by the time someone hires you—into an industry where receiving five hundred to a thousand résumés for any opening wasn't uncommon even long before the recession—you're expected to show up at the top of your game, even fresh out of school. Busy, distracted, and demanding bosses and hypercompetitive colleagues ensure that you quickly assume an air of knowing everything you need to, even if you can't even find the bathroom. You get good at faking it until you make it. It's not a business filled with warm, nurturing people who really want you to succeed. If you crash and burn, they can have your filing cabinet, your desk, and maybe even inherit your beat! In journalism, showing weakness, indecisiveness, or uncertainty was as ill-advised as walking around with toilet paper stuck to your shoe. No one would tell you how stupid you looked, and some would enjoy a good laugh at your expense.

Now, as I joined the legions of troops dedicated to sweater-folding and bag-filling, floor-sweeping and sizing, I wondered how complicated this job could actually *be*. How would they fill twenty-four hours with training?

At least they were paying us.

I looked around, curious to examine the group. Apart from Joe Fields, the manager who had interviewed me, I was the only Caucasian in the room. That was a first. My middle-class Toronto high school was almost exclusively white. My Canadian university, the University of Toronto, an extremely diverse school of fifty-three thousand students, and the nation's most competitive, had few minorities in my English, French, and Spanish classes. Only one of my journalism workplaces in thirty years, the *Daily News*, had included more than a handful of nonwhite faces. But here *I* was the visible minority.

Everyone was also twenty to thirty years younger than me.

I have good friends in their twenties and thirties, and have always gotten along well with people much younger. Even after I'd been married and divorced, changed countries a few times, and had some big jobs, my younger friends enjoyed and accepted me. We laughed at the same things, listened to some of the same music, enjoyed the same books. So I didn't fear working with people young enough to be one of my former students or interns. And, since I don't have kids, there was no chance of treating anyone as one of mine. Someone's age had never mattered as much to me as a relentless work ethic, a sense of humor, and mutual respect.

I'd also witnessed enough graybeards behaving like teenagers. At the *Daily News*, I sat near a man in his sixties, a legend in management's eyes and his own, who routinely shouted abuse at everyone, from his wife to fellow staffers. I knew, whatever someone's education, address, or work experience, nothing guaranteed considerate or professional behavior.

* * *

Several of the young women on our new team were whippet-lean, two of them model-gorgeous. Victoria, a college student who said she wanted to move into management, sported both a chin stud and bright-green-and-black-striped press-on nails. Almost everyone had a tattoo, and many had several. With only pierced ears and zero desire to ever get a tattoo, I felt dull, middle-aged, and suburban in comparison. For that reason alone, I wondered if they'd dismiss me as an old fogy, someone—literally—their mom's age.

One by one, we briefly introduced ourselves and explained why we wanted to work for this company. Their candor stunned me—at $9 an hour, I guess you could afford to be honest.

"I've been working at a supermarket in the meat department," said Bill. "I want to work somewhere warm."

"I've been working at Victoria's Secret," said Monique. "I'm sick of bras!"

I told the room I had no retail experience, and it was the first time in a very long time, maybe twenty years, that I'd been in a room full of people who knew a lot more about something than I did.

No one reacted. We all had a job, that's what counted. But why was everyone so passive? Almost no one asked questions. Were they incurious? Didn't they care? Of course, I was used to being around journalists. I began to realize that I'd been inhabiting a world in which information is oxygen and the ability to gather and process it both well and quickly is elemental to even basic survival, let alone success.

I felt like the fish in the old joke who's asked, "How's the water?"

And the fish says, "What water?"

Now, like a goldfish dumped from my familiar glass bowl, I was quite literally out of my depth.

Our days in training passed in an exhausting, overwhelming blur of product knowledge. We were each given a foot-thick binder, filled with detailed drawings and descriptions of the company's hundreds of boots, shoes, coats, jackets, shirts, and pants—and which models our store would be selling. It was hard to believe that there were so many iterations of nylon and fleece, so many variations of wind- and waterproofness.

Jacob, a genial thirty-year-old of Kenyan descent who worked in one of the Manhattan stores, was the product specialist taking us through it all. We passed around many of the actual garments and shoes. We even tried on some of them.

By day's end, our heads were bursting with the features and benefits of about three hundred items. We learned which ones were windproof, waterproof, wind-resistant, water-resistant. We learned what Gore-Tex was, how it worked, and why our customers should care. And we had to memorize a six-step sales process meant to take us seamlessly from our first encounter with a customer to our final words of thanks to them. We even role-played and were admonished never to annoy or alienate a customer—68 percent of a store's sales could be lost, we were told, if only one associate was rude, indifferent, or incompetent.

Was it true? Who knew?

None of us would have dared to challenge this statistic. Freshly hired into low-wage jobs, it simply wasn't our place to question authority. (Normally, I *would* have challenged any number so suspiciously specific. If I didn't, I'd be, and look like, a rube in a journalistic environment like a press conference surrounded by competitors, or even in a phone interview with a CEO or CFO with the PR flack listening in and protectively taping the exchange.) As we would learn in training, and in the years to come, such "statistics" are often just corporate jargon, a self-serving and usefully frightening management tool.

When I later ran this "official" number past a few industry experts, they laughed.

That I immediately felt so uncomfortable challenging such manufactured orthodoxy showed me I'd have to mute my lifelong skepticism and feistiness. It was clear that grilling managers, right now, and maybe later, would look obnoxious and possibly alienate my new coworkers. It would also slow the fire hose of data rushing at us. As a new team about to open a new store, it wasn't the time or place. We needed to form a cohesive unit *fast*, and we all knew it.

We'd become a platoon of soldiers prepping for battle—opening a new branch of a well-known store selling costly clothing in an affluent area just in time for the holidays—the C-130's rotor thudding impatiently in the background.

During our sessions, I'd been sitting beside Mark, a soft-spoken man hired as an assistant manager, who was clearly aware of our crucial role as the final deal-making link between this revered forty-year-old brand and its loyal customers. Sitting beside him every day, eating lunch from the salad bar at more-expensive but healthier Whole Foods while our younger colleagues rushed to McDonald's, I got to know him a bit. He'd come to The North Face with decades of experience working for H&M. He was weary of their blistering pace of product turnover and chaotic management style. Hungry for a change, he was eager to start anew with this respected company. He seemed serious, professional, and attentive.

But there was also Janice, a heavyset woman in her thirties, who had a chip on her shoulder from the beginning. On the final day of training she blurted out, "Don't be bringing your personal business to work!" (She was fired before the store opened, for being confrontational and rude to the managers. That, too, confirmed my first instinct to keep more of my opinions private.)

Shaniqua, newly remarried and pregnant with her fourth child at thirty, was stunningly beautiful, with a pixie haircut, stylish T-shirt, and wide eyes. Coolly confident, proudly showing her slightly swollen belly over the top of tight jeans, she demanded, "What's your maternity policy?"

I was most intrigued by Tameisha, a slim, quiet, self-contained black woman in her twenties, but wary of Carol, a short, fat, feisty college student. Like Janice, she had a hair-trigger temper, ready to turn on anyone who disagreed with her. Laura, a shy young woman, had been working at Fortunoff, a New York chain of jewelry and housewares stores. Her passive, polite manner seemed almost childlike in comparison to her peers, several of whom felt prematurely hardened and tough.

I asked so many questions that several people asked me if I was a manager. Partly it was my natural curiosity and partly my eagerness to do this new job really well. Mostly it was my nervousness about entering a field about whose inner workings I knew nothing. Shopping was one thing, selling another. Finally, I was asked to stop, as my curiosity was slowing the group's progress.

Phil Palmeri, a senior regional manager, trim and fit in a polo shirt and khakis, with a close-cropped fuzz of gray hair on his mostly bald head, spent a full day with us. This newest store was opening in a mall in the heart of a wildly affluent catchment area—one of the wealthiest regions in the United States. Our customers would be BlackBerry-wielding, foot-tapping high-earners and their stay-at-home wives, expecting deferential service. They'd come from towns like Greenwich, Darien, and Scarsdale, many of them neighborhoods with a *median* income of $140,000 or more and annual property taxes on their enormous homes exceeding $30,000, more than any full-time associate could ever hope to earn. We wouldn't ever get commissions, and would receive only minuscule raises and partial bonuses if and when we exceeded the store's sales goals, set and handed down from corporate headquarters far away.

Our managers didn't tell us any of this, even though knowing how incredibly demanding our customers would be might have weeded out some of the less polished associates more quickly. Experience working for a mass marketer like Victoria's Secret or H&M—their weary customers willing to tolerate long lines and few associates in exchange for cheap clothes—just wasn't enough. Even if we were only selling costly nylon and fleece, socks and running shoes and sleeping bags, our customers still demanded an extremely high level of service. They expected as much deference and product knowledge from us—earning no commission—for selling them an $80 backpack or $50 zip-neck fleece shirt as they would get if they were purchasing a $1,200 designer handbag or watch at Saks or Neiman Marcus.

Not to mention the cultural and socioeconomic chasm between this mall's shoppers and our staff. Our young associates might just as well be new immigrants from some distant Pacific island when it came to shared experiences with the drawling skinny blondes and cashmere-sweatered corporate attorneys we'd be serving. Few of our associates had traveled, even domestically, while our customers were jetting off to Aspen, Park City, the Galápagos, or Chile. It was a safe bet most of our shoppers had never visited Yonkers, Harlem, or Washington Heights, the neighbor-hoods—largely lower-income and minority-inhabited—where most of our new staff lived.

I'd been living in this county for twenty years and had occasionally shopped at this mall; I knew these people. They were my neighbors, if not my social circle.

In journalism, the role of reporters as corporate ambassadors was rarely acknowledged. Here, I was struck by how differently these man-agers were treating us, workers who were relatively uneducated and technically disposable, near the bottom of the wage scale. The mood was one of consistent, calm professionalism, something I'd rarely glimpsed in my own field. At the *Daily News*, one British manager—editor in chief Martin Dunn—almost never spoke to reporters, only to his most senior deputies, the vast majority of them male. He strode the length of the newsroom, whistling in his made-to-order suits, as disdainful of the skilled and hardworking writers filling his pages every day as a Dicken-sian factory owner would be of the youngsters bent dutifully over their machines.

In the four days we spent getting to know The North Face and its history and products, only one person struck me as a robo-corporate type, the LP expert, a woman who had flown in from the head office in California. LP, I learned, stood for loss prevention—that is, shoplifting and internal theft. We were warned about a fairly dazzling array of theft techniques, some of which could even foil the thick beige plastic sensor tags that I had always assumed were unassailable. Not so.

First, she told us not to tackle a thief. Who would? Then she warned us, in plain language, not to steal from the company. We would always be visible on store cameras, the tapes available for review by trained experts, providing excellent evidence for arrest and prosecution.

"We know all the tricks," she told us. "We've seen them all. You *will* be caught and you *will* be fired."

Nice vote of confidence. I had never worked in an environment where theft of anything valuable was an option. Notebooks and pens, tools of the writer's trade, weren't worth much on the open market. This level of mistrust going into a new job felt intrusive and ugly. I understood it from a business perspective, but it struck a dissonant note when we were supposed to be building solidarity with one another and some sense of loyalty to our new employer.

If we weren't deemed trustworthy, why hire us? It sent a lousy message and a warning of future micromanagement, a reminder that this was, after all, a crummy low-wage job and we had few choices or we wouldn't be here. And, since we had so few choices, I guess the logic went, of course we'd be more likely to steal from the company.

By our final night of training, we were starting to feel like a team, and the company treated us to a sit-down dinner at the hotel. We were celebrating our graduation after long days sitting in a stuffy conference room memorizing reams of data about the firm, its products, and how to sell them. My employers in journalism has never welcomed me with a dinner, or even a meal. The day I began at the *Daily News* I sat in the lobby for forty-five minutes before anyone acknowledged I was there. And I was once interviewed in Manhattan for an editor-in-chief position in a private suite at the Carlyle, one of the world's costliest and most elegant hotels, by an Irish media mogul—the magazine's publisher—who never even offered me coffee.

Phil, our district manager, joined us for the entire meal. He was warm and down-to-earth. He engaged us in real conversation, listened carefully, and seemed genuinely interested in our cautious, polite replies. You could tell from the associates' reactions this level of respect and interest was extremely unusual in such a low-level job. Why was he being so nice to us? However calculated, it made a powerful and positive first impression.

I assumed we'd never see Phil again. But we did, every three or four months, when he would drop in to the store, one of sixteen he was then responsible for.

Two associates, giggling like naughty schoolchildren at their audacious selection, each ordered the $28 sirloin.

"When else can we eat like this?" they asked the rest of us, daring us to do the same. Instead, most of us ordered modestly, a burger or a salad. On our combined income from journalism, steak was not as much of a luxury for Jose and me—we ate it a few times a month. And yet, compared to my middle-aged friends and neighbors, most of whom had high six-figure combined incomes, I often felt like a loser.

"Are you still writing?" they'd ask me brightly, as though my life's profession were a hobby, something I did to fill the time and earn a little play money. These fellow suburbanites, the wealthiest certainly, owned multiple homes, vacationed lavishly, and groomed their kids attending private school for the Ivy League. They drove new Lexuses and Mercedes and BMWs. Skinny blond wives happily stayed at home to manage their kids and enormous mansions. They had no idea what to make of me.

Now, sitting at this hotel dinner table, surrounded by my new colleagues whose choices and experiences had been so different from mine—their tattoos and piercings, their hollow gold door-knocker earrings, hoodies, and skin-tight clothes—I wondered where, if anywhere, I belonged. I was beginning to appreciate the cocoon I'd been living in until then. In our co-op building, everyone owned their home. I attended a church whose parishioners were wealthy lawyers, network TV anchors and producers, Wall Street money guys. The people I knew socially and professionally drove late-model cars and vacationed overseas. My new coworkers lived in lower-income neighborhoods far away from the mall, like Washington Heights at the north end of Manhattan, or the Bronx, just slightly farther south than where we were, who would be commuting an hour or more by bus each way to the new store, some of whom were raising three and four children on an hourly wage of $9 to $11 an hour.

I turned to Dave, a poised, good-looking eighteen-year-old college student, who told me that he was on a basketball scholarship and wrote poetry. Our conversation flowed easily. He was smooth, polished, charming. We both loved Sandra Cisneros, and I offered to lend him a book of poems by my favorite, Yeats, someone he had never heard of.

* * *

Reality hit. Our new store was still being built, so we couldn't train there. Instead, we trekked into Manhattan to train on the sales floor of their larger store for two days. It felt like a combined field trip and audition. Except we'd already been hired.

I was acutely aware that everyone but me had already worked retail, some of them for years. To stand for hours on end without a break, to engage total strangers in successful sales transactions, was no big deal to any of them.

It was to me! I was scared to death.

I rarely sweat with anxiety, but the first time I approached a customer (couldn't they tell I had no experience?) I sure did.

The mix of customers was wild: tourists from Austria, Switzerland, New Zealand, three burly city sanitation workers looking for sturdy and comfortable work boots. The day's first customer? Actress Janine Turner, former star of one of my favorite television series, *Northern Exposure*. She bought a suitcase and filled it with $1,000 worth of merchandise. Dave was lucky enough to help her, although I called her by name and helped carry her bags to the curb. She was lovely, down-to-earth, and chatty.

I was now as anonymous as my fellow coworkers. In my usual journalist's role, a presumed social equality was part of the game, and I wouldn't have hesitated to introduce myself, tell Janine I was a fan, and speak to her socially, maybe ask her some questions. Not now. It was simply not my place. A retail associate is there to sell product, support the brand, and be invisibly helpful.

A couple from Scarsdale, he a lawyer, she a stay-at-home mom—who said they couldn't wait for our suburban new store to open—spent $3,000 on a towering pile of clothes for themselves and their kids. (This remains the single largest sale I saw during my entire time at The North Face.)

The Manhattan store was huge, more than four times larger than the one we'd be working in. Just going into its stockroom was exhausting, running up and down a narrow flight of stairs dozens of times a day, not to mention scaling the tall staircase from the main floor to the second floor. I wondered how anyone working there lasted physically through their shifts—our store, at least, was going to be compact and all on one level.

On our second and final day before the opening, Mark tried to climb the stockroom stairs and doubled over in agony, his narrow face suddenly twisting in pain. The pain in his groin was piercing and relentless, he whispered to me. He never returned to work and ended up in the hospital for weeks. Despite my repeated requests for information about him, my manager wouldn't give me any details. He would live, I was told, but Mark had left the state to recuperate with his parents. It was clear that we wouldn't be seeing him again.

Meanwhile, I had no idea where anything was and tried to memorize the merchandise so that when a customer asked for help, I could actually offer it. We were taught how to use the cash register. I watched Jacob swoosh credit cards through it with practiced ease and wondered if I'd ever be so confident.

In a quiet moment, I had a chance to speak privately with Paul, the store's assistant manager, whose eyes were so dark that the pupils were almost indistinguishable from the irises. Short, trim, and handsome, with a distinctive, attractive modesty, he'd once danced professionally in a major American ballet company. As we shared our pre-retail histories, we discovered this unlikely commonality. I had studied ballet for years. We compared our favorite choreographers, and then, it turned out, I learned he'd also lived and worked, as I had, in France. There, he had worked as a chef, and before that had led a group of soldiers in the French Foreign Legion. Workaholic journalists, most scared to even leave their desks for lunch for fear of losing their hard-to-win jobs, *never* had such cool stories.

I wondered what other surprises lurked beneath the exterior of my new colleagues.

* * *

Finally, our store was ready.

It was in an odd location in the mall, at the end of a long line of stores for babies and children I called Kiddies' Row. When I shopped there—which was rare—I avoided this section entirely to avoid the screaming kids, weary moms, and their oversized strollers clogging the aisles. Given our store's focus on outdoor clothing for athletic adults, with only a tiny selection for ages three through twelve, I wondered if our older customers would ever find us. There was no local advertising to give them any clue that we were opening or where we were. And since we weren't facing a street, we couldn't hang out a banner or distribute leaflets on the corner. But we *were* situated just across the hall from the Apple store, whose hip young customers were a good fit for us. And we were a few doors away from four other stores with appropriate demographics: Hollister, Anthropologie, Pottery Barn, and Crate & Barrel.

Hundreds of heavy boxes started pouring in, the stock we'd have to sort, tag, sensor, fold, stack, and hang. The space was brilliantly lit with enormous industrial-looking lights, the raw concrete walls lined with a blackened steel shelving system whose configurations we could change and move at will. The placement of merchandise—typical of national chains—allowed no room for chance, improvisation, or creativity, as thick binders of photographs and charts sent out from the head office dictated where everything must go. The clothing was chosen for us as well as how it would be displayed. Regional tastes or differences? Not interested.

We would soon be able to tell, within minutes of unpacking yet another shipment of this preselected *shmatta*, what would never, ever sell to our customers: skimpy little dresses, floppy skirts, brown polyester "jean" jackets with pink stitching, almost anything produced in white or cream fabric.

Yet, according to the head office—aka "corporate"—every store had to maintain a look totally consistent with every other North Face store in the country, as if anyone outside the company would notice or care. The Manhattan store, which had a spectacular carved wooden bench from Tibet at its entrance during our training and a hand-carved dark wood Tibetan cabinet being used for display, was soon stripped of these excessively quirky, noncorporate choices. This despite North Face's mantra of exploration, a message bolstered by enormous colored photographs we'd prop up everywhere around the store, of their sponsored athletes climbing and trekking and doing yoga in cool, exotic places like . . . Tibet.

That humorless, central-command rigidity also left a powerful impression on me. It was an attitude I'd see more and more as time went by.

The shelves of our new store were pale striated bamboo, the floor a gleaming dark wood. A few areas were marked off with red and gray carpet tile, adding color and texture. Each of the two dressing rooms included an elegant wooden Eames chair.

Three cash registers sat on the cash wrap, the long dark steel counter where we faced our customers to collect their money and wrap or bag their purchases. Another long steel credenza stood behind it, its drawers and cupboards holding the tools of the trade: price guns, Lucite folding boards in men's, women's, and children's sizes, beige tissue paper, shiny red North Face stickers, gray cardboard gift boxes, warranty cards, layaway cards, and the paperwork for "charge-sends" (used to order from another store and ship directly to the client's home). With every detail custom-made, it was a pleasure to use bamboo drawers that glided easily and cabinets faced with smooth wooden panels that opened and closed with a quiet click. (On my first day at the *Daily News*, I was ushered to my desk and given, with no apology or explanation, a computer with a keyboard so crusted with food and drink that I didn't want to touch it. My black office-style chair was dirty, the fabric torn, and the seat itself leaning and broken. I opened my desk drawer to discover a pair of filthy, smelly men's running shoes, left behind by the last occupant, whom they'd fired.)

It might not sound like much, but when you're working in any environment for hours on end, it matters a lot if it's too hot, poorly lit, cluttered and messy, or tasteful and inviting. This store's sales floor, at least, had been seriously thought through. Enormous color photos of lean athletes doing dangerous things in exotic locations—hiking in Chile, doing yoga in rural China—were propped high above us, a reminder of what this brand was supposed to be all about: exploration, adventure, risk-taking, achievement.

The contrast between the sales floor and the employees-only area was stark, if unsurprising; as a shopper, I'd glimpsed the scuffed, dingy walls behind the scenes at Saks and Lord & Taylor. Our clothing stockroom was probably twenty feet high, lined with two long double-height rows of vertically stacked beige metal racks. The shelves above them were stuffed with huge, heavy cardboard boxes, unreachable without using a heavy, tall folding ladder. In front of these stood rolling garment racks, which rendered the racks behind them invisible and slowed ready access to the clothes. A second stockroom was jammed floor to ceiling with more metal shelves holding boxes of boots and shoes, pegboards for gloves and hats, more shelves crammed with luggage and sleeping bags and backpacks, shopping bags and gift boxes, and display materials.

I was so ready for this job to start. I was hungry for distraction, something new and demanding.

We were issued name tags, our first names carved into a square of red and white plastic and worn on a red cotton lanyard with the store's name printed on it. I'd never worn a name tag at work, only at conferences where I was an honored speaker whose words were taped and sold, sometimes even quoted back to me years later by a listener who found them helpful.

Then we were given our company uniforms, pieces from the fall 2007 collection; for women, a nylon quarter-zip shirt, one in light blue, one in brown, and a pair of white mesh sneakers with thick black soles. They weren't great-looking, but they were comfortable, light, and breathable and offered good support. We could wear what we wanted as trousers but no blue jeans or sweatpants.

There were tiny lockers—maybe a foot square—in which, only during our shift, we could store our things. We could not eat or drink or chew gum in front of the customers, nor could we leave any drink containers on top of our lockers. No one would see them but us. Why would it matter? *It didn't.*

We'd get an hour's break each shift, unpaid—the only one we'd have in a seven- or eight-hour period. We were not allowed to sit down in view of the customers and certainly were not encouraged to do so anywhere else. The sales floor had only one place to sit, a slatted bamboo bench in front of the shoe wall at the rear of the store. State labor law mandated only one thirty-minute meal break for a full shift, so there was no official respite until our meal break arrived. (We'd learn, instead, to sit on the toilet for a lot longer and more frequently than physically necessary, just for some privacy and the chance to send a text or check e-mail or call someone.)

The break area was simply a slab of Formica nailed to one end of the stockroom with a microwave on it and a half-refrigerator below. The mall's food court was nearby, at the top of the escalators, but its choices were limited and expensive. I was one of the very few—perhaps the only one—who consistently bought food and ate it there. A food court meal could easily run $8 or $12, an hour of hard, sweaty labor squandered. Most of my coworkers bought a Big Mac or a slice of pizza nearby and ate in the break room.

Each of us was assigned a six-digit employee number that we'd use to log on to the computer's time clock to record when we arrived and left, and when we began and ended our meal breaks. I was now 431877. I'd never even seen a time clock—most of my newsroom and magazine jobs began around ten a.m., and no one ever visibly kept tabs on us. I might be gone for days at a time, checking in only by e-mail or cell phone, but my boss was certain of a story at the end of it all.

Journalists with staff jobs thrived, most of us, on a specific and much-appreciated blend of corporate solidity and autonomy. Our paychecks would clear, we'd have a desk and chair and phone and voice mail, we had bosses and colleagues and maybe even interns. We each had business cards, a tool we took for granted. Here, in retail, only after you'd sold tens of thousands in merchandise would the company award you $30 worth of personalized cards.

Depending on where we worked as journalists, we often also enjoyed considerable personal independence, the cherished freedom to flee the bonds of the office and its routines, gossip, and politics, for hours, even days or weeks at a time, while working on an approved story. The editors knew that some of the most important stories could take a long time to produce. So you often didn't find the best reporters sitting in the newsroom; the most trusted veterans among them were almost always invisible. They were out there, somewhere, doing their job.

Retail's level of control, scrutiny, and uniformity felt weird, both infantilizing and excessive. Typical of the industry, we had to show a manager the contents of our purses and shopping bags every single time we left the store, even for our breaks. We had to tell someone we were *going* on our break even when it was clearly marked on the schedule before we arrived that day. "Dinner" might come at four p.m.—but we wouldn't leave the store until nine-thirty or nine forty-five p.m. That was a long time between meals, let alone our only chance to simply sit still and rest quietly for a few minutes.

I disliked being so monitored, de facto distrusted before we'd even done anything wrong.

Writers live for recognition, readers, remembrance. Since college, my name—so unusual then that many readers assumed it was a euphonious pseudonym—had for years been my career calling card. It was my by-line, the indelible marker through which, for decades, editors and readers and colleagues knew me. Now my name was carved into a piece of plastic, I was assumed to be a potential criminal, reduced to a six-digit sales code, and my task was to serve hundreds of strangers while being constantly monitored by Big Brother.

If I fixed my bra strap or blew my nose or simply stood still to catch my breath, no matter how I was feeling—whether sharing a joke with a coworker or trying not to snap at a rude customer—my face, my reactions, my tone and language were completely visible, caught on one of the store's many cameras—and a manager sitting in his minuscule office was viewing it all. Who else could, or would, review their tapes as well?

Welcome to a low-wage, low-skill job. Intense oversight and prescriptive behavior were just a few of its many costs.

I chatted up associates at a few other stores in this upscale mall, people I'd previously taken for granted while a shopper myself, but now people who could offer me, a retail novice in their midst, the keys to the kingdom. They knew how things worked.

One woman my age told me her company demanded certain tasks be completed by a specific time every day. She wasn't working in some fluorescent-lit discount cavern like Walmart, but a high-end stationery chain whose products I'd long admired and often purchased. I had never before considered the working conditions of these companies, naïvely assuming that a place devoted to the art of communicating with elegance and style would treat its employees with the same graciousness its products were designed to convey. I would soon learn that many respected companies' labor practices were much less pleasant than my fantasies. I had long loved their beautiful products and attractive stores. Now—having peeked behind the curtain, as it were—I saw this company less favorably. The more I began to learn about some of these companies, whose pockets I'd happily lined for years as a shopper, and the careless corporate brutality with which they treated their associates, the less I liked them.

Now, when I saw an associate, of any age, race, or gender, I no longer saw "them."

I saw "us."

The more I got to know the other stores in the mall, most of them large national or international chains, the more I also got to know some of the people working in them when I stopped in on my break to buy a bar of soap or a bottle of nail polish. The more I heard from their workers, now comrades-in-arms—long hours, unpredictable shifts, abusive customers, shockingly heavy workloads, and, of course, no commission—the less I admired these companies. I no longer browsed their dreamy catalogs or elaborate Web sites quite so avidly. I realized, belatedly, they were also workplaces, not just a fun spot for me and others to drop some cash or while away a half hour.

What I saw was often depressing.

Rigidity may be efficient, but I quickly saw how unhappy it made the frontline workers. And workers who aren't happy, believe it, take it out on their customers. I always dreaded, and generally avoided for that reason, shopping at my local Kmart, no matter how great its prices, so utterly miserable, and so few, were its clerks.

I confided to this woman in the stationery store that I was new to the physical demands of retail work. I asked her quietly, woman-to-woman of a certain age, how she could stand for hours at a time without dropping from fatigue. I was too proud and embarrassed to ask my own colleagues, all of whom were so young that stamina surely wasn't an issue for them.

"You'll get used to it," she told me sympathetically. "It'll happen suddenly one day, overnight. You'll have weeks of pain and think you can't take it anymore. Then, all of a sudden, it just stops hurting."

* * *

Our on-the-floor training, all two days of it, was over.

It was showtime.

Journalists, some of whom had invested their time, money, and egos in costly Ivy League undergraduate and graduate degrees, often complained ferociously about how hard they worked for much lower pay than their friends in law and medicine—that is, the "professions." They moaned when their editors demanded too much or when their copy was messed with. Cynical and skeptical, by nature or training, they were typically a grouchy, prickly crowd.

They had no idea. This kind of work was hard in a whole new way. I wondered if any one of them would last a week behind the cash wrap.

It was tiring. I'd worked long hours before. At the *Daily News*, I'd done a stakeout for two long days in midtown Manhattan in eighty-degree heat and humidity. In Montreal's winter, I'd reported stories outdoors in subzero temperatures, trying to juggle pen, notebook, and thick gloves. But no matter how rough the gig, I'd always had some control over when I could rest, even for five minutes.

No more. Just going to the toilet, having the chance to sit for a few moments in privacy and silence, quickly became a welcome treat. Between the store's blazing hot lights and schlepping stock, much of it heavy, bulky jackets, and running back and forth to the stockrooms, I was often drenched in sweat, my official nylon shirt stinky within hours.

It was dehydrating. I'd never seen straight men moisturize before, certainly not in public, but we all learned quickly the only way to protect our skin from cracking and bleeding was by lubing up regularly. Handling fabric all day long leached the moisture from our skin, so badly my fingertips cracked and bled. Picking garbage off the floor and touching germ-laden cash, credit cards, phones, and other objects also meant using hand sanitizer or soap and hot water several times a day as we tried to stay healthy.

Everyone kept cups of soda, water, tea, or coffee handy, sipping or gulping whenever possible, although company rules forbade us from doing so in front of customers. Hot lights and nonstop physical activity left us thirsty.

It was emotionally draining. Whatever the customer demanded, no matter how unreasonable or impossible, you'd better give it quickly and without hesitation. The nasty ones—who were almost always female—would get even nastier if you paused or slowed down or weren't sure or, worst of all, raised an eyebrow.

It was tedious. We were each assigned a section of the L-shaped store, one of three zones for which we were solely responsible that day. It was up to each of us to make sure that area was clean, organized, tidy, well stocked, and that every single item was displayed in size order. Secret shoppers sent by the corporate head office could descend at any time without warning, as did some of our senior outside managers. If any one of us screwed up, all of us could lose potential shared bonuses or worse.

It meant scutwork. The company was getting a lot for its money, because they wouldn't hire a cleaning crew. We were it, which meant dusting all the shelves, sweeping and mopping the dark wood floor, polishing the five tall mirrors, vacuuming the carpet tiles, removing smudges from the shoe mirrors, front doors, and display cases. Even cleaning the toilets (and signing a sheet to prove we had all taken a turn doing so). I confess, I never did it and was never chastised for not doing it. Like some of my coworkers, I found the idea demeaning. No one ever said anything to me, although some must have noticed my name never went up on that sign-up sheet. It was my one, really my only, way to rebel without losing my job.

Many of our customers were people whose messes—and those of their children—were picked up uncomplainingly by a silent army of maids and nannies and au pairs. They thought nothing of trashing the joint. I scraped chewing gum off the floor, found pieces of food underneath clothes left in piles, and discovered countless half-filled bottles or paper cups full of sticky soda or coffee ready to spill all over the merchandise.

It was becoming quickly obvious that the actual work of keeping the store clean would cost us face-time with customers, reducing our sales and making it tougher to achieve our individual daily sales goals, which could reach into the high four figures. No wonder there were dust bunnies the size of armadillos.

It was hazardous. While the sales floor was welcoming and attractive, the three stockrooms and narrow hallways leading into them were a disaster waiting to happen. Sensor pins an inch long were forever scattered on the floor. Plastic bags discarded on the linoleum invited a slip or slide into something sharp. Half-opened or discarded cardboard boxes and garment racks blocked our movement. There was absolutely no way, without finding, lugging, setting up, and climbing a heavy folding stepladder, for someone my height—five-foot-five—to reach even the bottom of the second hanging rack. I couldn't read the tags on anything hanging there in order to find a size. If the tags were hanging, as some did, from the collar, it was impossible without making the time to clamber up there and check. Above the top of that rack were huge cardboard boxes of additional stock stacked two and three high. There was no way I was going to climb up there like a monkey, risking life and limb, for $11 an hour.

I started to loathe any customer who asked to see a pair of boots or shoes. The boxes were heavy and unwieldy and their dollar value low for the physical effort and additional time it took to sell them. Not to mention the shoe and boot stockroom was so poorly lit we could barely read the labels. The central aisle, stacked floor to ceiling with boots and shoes, was so dim we strained to see anything, slowing us down unnecessarily. That annoyed toe-tapping shoppers, who would sigh or look impatiently and pointedly at their watches when we finally returned.

And while the store was an attractive place to work, the mall's ventilation system was a joke—we would dust everything to perfection at one p.m. and within a few hours a new layer of sediment had resettled on everything.

Welcome to the Augean stables.

* * *

We opened in late October, giving us barely a month to settle in before the Christmas rush. If we were not totally on our game, cooperating smoothly, each of us equally knowledgeable about our hundreds of products with the ability to locate them all really fast, things could get ugly.

No pressure.

We were beginning to see who was reliable, who called in sick—in retail parlance "calling out"—who came in late, who was a diva, and who never dusted or cleaned.

A neat freak, I'd already gained a reputation as something of a suck-up because I was always cleaning. I hated dirt and dust, to which I was allergic. I wanted to work in a clean space, and customers paying $600 for a ski jacket might realistically expect the same.

So I was usually the one wielding the Windex bottle, clambering up the folding aluminum ladder we dragged all over the store to dust the fifteen frosted-glass shelves of the shoe wall or reaching deep beneath a rack of ski pants to grab fist-sized clumps of black lint. It wasn't that I loved cleaning that much (although I enjoy housework at home), but sitting around doing nothing when there were no customers was boring. After you'd sorted everything into size order, there was simply nothing left to do but reread the product catalog, memorize more numbing details, or gossip with your colleagues.

I admit, this was where things broke down for me. I wasn't twenty and I didn't listen to rap and hip-hop or watch BET, or have kids, so it wasn't easy to find common ground with the teens and moms among us.

I knew I seemed cold and standoffish. But, other than gender and our employer, I had few experiences they could relate to, and vice versa.

And I was really uncomfortable with the behavior of a few of the youngest associates, girls who giggled loudly with one another, shrieking out song lyrics within earshot and sight lines of customers. I was amazed that no one disciplined them.

Better I should clean and stay busy.

* * *

Now that the mall was my new workplace, even one or two days a week, I began to see it with fresh eyes.

We think we're just going shopping. Maybe it's for something we really need, right now, or maybe we're out for a stroll, idly wandering a favorite street and poking in and out of stores, vaguely seeking the perfect . . . *something* . . . that makes us decide to own it. It might be a cupcake or a pair of sneakers or a new sofa. We may think we're in charge, as so many shoppers now first research their purchases online, or text and photograph their desired items in the store and wait for a friend's or parent's approval before buying them. But those who design stores, and especially those planning and conceptualizing the malls that contain them, know better.

"You're trying to build a better mousetrap," says Peter Tovell, a Toronto architect whose thirty-year career has been devoted to designing malls and shopping centers. "It's a phrase we use all the time. We don't want you to be able to find your way out! Our job is to create a whole different world."

Other than Anthropologie, only one store in our mall was different from all the rest in its design, J. Jill. Like Anthropologie, J. Jill's stores and catalogs offer a carefully curated aesthetic, their comfortable, loose-fitting women's clothes most often manufactured of linen, cotton, wool, or other natural fibers in soothing tones of taupe, sky-blue, pale ame-thyst, butter-yellow, light gray. You won't find bright red or loud prints or tight-fitting tank tops there. Everything is gentle, cozy, many products with elastic-band waists, forgiving of thicker, middle-aged flesh.

Even the entrance to their store is unusual: smooth rounded pebbles as flooring; silvery door handles that look like birch limbs, double wooden doors with glass inserts, and, inside, simple white glass and matte silvery metal wall sconces. In contrast to almost every other store in the mall, their space is soothing, with low lighting and comfortable chairs.

While some retailers dismiss the notion that good store design mat-ters to shoppers, others feel passionately that it matters a great deal.

Monocle, a monthly magazine devoted to the global good life, edited by Canadian-born taste arbiter Tyler Brûlé, annually chooses its retail stars worldwide. Their favorites for 2010 include The Department Store, in Auckland, New Zealand, which sells clothing, interior design prod-ucts, and contains a café and a hair salon within a repurposed post office. In Tokyo, shoppers at Gunze can customize cotton and nylon under-pants using Macs in the store's basement to tweak more than a million choices. Not surprisingly, given Brûlé's professed love of Japanese retail, nine of the magazine's top twenty-five are in Tokyo. At MaPharmacie, on the rue des Tournelles in Paris, Michael Zazoun, a pharmacist with a business degree, made a bold, playful and unusual choice for his store, with its strikingly handsome green stone tile floor, by covering the door to his stockroom with plants. "I love seeing the customers when we come out," he told *Monocle*. "They always smile."

"A lot of retailers believe environment is neutral—we think presenta-tion is just as important [as the products we display]," says Urban Out-fitters CEO Glen Senk. His company owns Anthropologie; in a vicious recession when almost every other retailer was closing stores, slashing inventory, and firing executives, their sales grew by 22 percent to $1.8 billion. That's a lot of smelly soap and lacy camisoles.

Every Apple store creates its own brand of visual excitement, the store an enormous glass box filled with white walls, counters, and floors, and smart, geeky young sales staff. The store itself is a simulacrum of a MacBook or iPad—a sleek, glossy, sexy toy you just can't wait to play with, let alone show off.

Malls these days are doing whatever they can to stay relevant, trying to woo high-spending consumers who—unlike a few years ago—aren't Baby Boomers, now worried about retirement and paying for their kids' college, but teens and tweens who live at home and still have plenty of disposable income as a result.

"Every mall in America is desperate for newness and freshness," Jim Fielding, president of Disney Stores Worldwide, told *The New York Times* in October 2009 as the company planned a total renovation of its 340 stores in the United States and Europe. "We will essentially be the only toy retailer left at the mall because everybody else has evaporated," said Andy Mooney, chairman of Disney Consumer Products. So eager is Disney to reboot its brand, it turned to Steve Jobs, whose Apple stores typically throng with eager shoppers. "Dream bigger," was his retail advice.

By September 2009, mall vacancy rates nationwide hit 8.4 percent, the highest level since commercial real estate firm Reis began keeping statistics a decade earlier. At Concord Mall in Elkhart, Indiana, a 4,900-square-foot space, once a toy store and unoccupied for four years, is now home to the evangelical FreshStart Church. In Nashville, the One Hundred Oaks Mall welcomed the Vanderbilt Medical Center, 436,000 square feet—almost half the building's space.

To make everyone happy, says Tovell, mall owners now offer plenty of soft seating and higher-end washrooms. Amenities like trees and fountains (which our mall had) are now considered passé.

"A retail design is only good for seven or eight years," he says. "Your merchandise can change, but the store has to change as well or people will just think it's the same old stuff as before."

Key to pulling shoppers into a mall, and keeping them there, is making sure there are safe, clean, comfortable spots to rest. "Food courts now look like restaurants and have soft seating," he says. (Our food court, in sad contrast, had only hard chairs and televisions blaring constantly.)

Ever notice the bathroom ceiling in a mall? You'll never see acoustic tiles—the light, movable squares lifted out of the way in suspense movies so someone can hide there. That's because they also would provide a great place to stash drugs and facilitate dealing, one kind of commerce no mall owner wants to attract or encourage, Tovell says.

Malls, in general, have become dinosaurs—too big, too boring, too sterile, too exhausting to maneuver. And, with more than 40 million Americans suffering some form of arthritis, even navigating the long halls of most malls can offer a wearying and dispiriting ordeal. When it hurts to walk, maneuvering any significant distance makes shopping a chore.

"The industry has really nosedived in the past two or three years. We only did two or three," Tovell explains. "The new thing is 'community centers.' They're very successful and very cheap to build. They have a grocery store and a drugstore and a bank. Social interaction is very important and they have to be *safe*. Sight lines are very important: no hidden corners, no stairwells, much higher ceilings, and much brighter lighting."

Mall design is often a contradiction in terms, Tovell admits. "There's a standard prototype and they get lazy and keep using it over and over and over again. They do it on the cheap."

What mall owners and operators do care about, he says, is safety, making shoppers feel cared for. "Security is huge. It's practically the driving force right now. They're using cameras like crazy. Security is something they put out front and center. Right at the entrance to a mall, you'll see a sign reading 'Security Office.'"

Not every mall is as boring as the one I worked in—one South African mall has a drive-in theater on its roof and another has a high school sports stadium incorporated into its space.

While staying with a friend near Peterborough, a middle-class central Ontario city of 74,000, in November 2010, I visited Lansdowne Place, a thirty-one-year-old mall undergoing renovation. Just as Tovell describes, the center was anchored by a major pharmacy and a grocery superstore. I had never seen a mall space so well-designed or so inviting. Soft banquette seating with attractive upholstery anchored the food court's perimeter, while the tables and chairs serving its 268 diners were stylishly made of pale wood. The floor tile was a soft, creamy white with rough edges, the kind you might choose for your own bathroom or kitchen. Even on a gloomy fall afternoon, the space still enjoyed plenty of natural light from many large clerestory windows. The room's soaring Craftsman-style wood columns in a warm mahogany color created an unusually sophisticated and much more welcoming atmosphere than the usual cold white paint or gleaming marble of older malls.

But the food court's most striking and alluring feature was a large, round central fireplace, gas-fired, its curved glass walls sheathed by a metal vine, its flames easily visible from across a room the length of a football field. Shoppers of all ages gravitated to the hearth, nestling deep within large leather armchairs or rust-colored upholstered wing chairs. Conversation could flow easily between strangers enjoying a relaxing break from shopping.

And what more powerful symbol of shared comfort in a rural area where winter is fierce, isolating, and long than a beautifully presented communal fire?

Happily surprised by all this unexpected beauty, I sat there for more than two hours.

We're rarely indifferent to malls, no matter how much we mock, or revere, them. They arouse powerful reactions; when architecture critic Alison Arieff wrote about them in June 2009 in *The New York Times*, 265 readers weighed in. One reader deplored "gum-chewing zombies with tattoos and piercings at the cash register." Many complained that traditional malls are too big, too sterile, and simply exhausting, forcing shoppers to wander in circles searching for parking, a seat, or simply the exit. One writer in Shanghai said every major mall in that city has a grocery store and drugstore: "Doing errands has never been more convenient."

(I grew up taking this sort of retail mix—common in Toronto and Montreal's many underground shopping complexes—for granted. They're a great, comfortable solution to long, cold, snowy winters and hot, humid summers, allowing shoppers to walk comfortably indoors for miles without ever having to exit.)

The mall where I worked was hopeless in this regard, all big name designers or mass market chain stores. Even as a shopper, I avoided it because it annoyed me so much to pay to park. Even Paco Underhill, who's probably spent more time (professionally) shopping than anyone, says, "Most malls are twenty-five years or older and they were butt ugly when they opened and they haven't gotten any prettier."

No matter where you shop, you're quarry, potential big game to be approached—quickly, cheerfully, discreetly—within ten seconds or ten feet of an associate. That was our rule, anyway, and one fairly common in the industry. Because no matter your branding, design, marketing, and advertising or how many bodies you pull into your carefully designed store with its specially chosen Muzak, they're worthless until they're ready to spend some money.

That's our job.

The associate's task, in retail parlance, is also a religious one—conversion. Only by thoughtfully approaching and carefully managing each customer can associates successfully convert them from looking to buying, trying their best to make sure they eventually purchase something.

Paco Underhill's firm Envirosell, hired by major malls and retailers around the world, from South Africa to Brazil to Canada, tracks shoppers so minutely it's a little creepy. With the use of thousands of metrics, customers are videotaped and listened to and watched and trailed by experts with detailed spreadsheets noting every possible interaction with every aspect of the store. When they entered, did they pause? Turn left? Pick up a shopping basket or a cart? Did they read the signage? To do so, did they have to squint or raise their head?

Worst of all, did a fellow shopper shove them? (The dreaded "butt brush" sends female shoppers to the exit, his research shows. People don't want to feel a stranger's flesh hitting them when they're in the zone, lost in thought and trying to decide what, if anything, to buy.) Destroy that valuable reverie at your peril!

Conversion remains the golden, precious, and elusive point of the whole exercise. It's a shimmering, bobbing, fragile soap bubble of trust, curiosity, amusement, and discovery that, briefly, envelops and joins seller and possible buyer. One fake smile, an unanswered question, an overeager upsell—and, *pop!*, you've lost it for good. Like many shoppers, I've walked out of stores, annoyed by incompetence and resentful at my wasted time, after someone has tried too hard to *sell*. In one chic Madison Avenue boutique, two male associates practically jumped me the minute I entered the store, and I rebuffed them. Later, away from the owner—who, they confided, insisted they sell so hard—they apologized. "We hate pushing like that," they told me. But, we all knew, they also wanted to keep their jobs, no matter how annoying their style.

Just as bad are careless or disinterested associates, one of whom prompted a funny, too-true rant in *The New York Times* by David Sax, a young Brooklyn journalist who went out—fruitlessly—in search of a new suit:

"I'm sorry. Didn't mean to interrupt your text messaging, which is probably what brought that look of scorn to your face, but I was wondering if you could help me . . . Each time I open my mouth to ask you a question about the clothes you're selling, your nose scrunches, your eyes roll, and your head darts down to where the register is. I can't imagine what's so pressing. I'm the only customer here."

THREE
FITTING IN

My new job wasn't just a paycheck.

Instead, it demanded new and unfamiliar ways of thinking—about customers, managers, coworkers, and myself. After decades as a news journalist, well paid and intellectually valued for my willingness to challenge and question authority, it was now my role to defer, serve, and obey. I'd chosen journalism, and done well in it, because part of our job was poking a finger in the eye of the pompous and wealthy, the powerful and overpraised.

Now I'd be kowtowing to them instead.

Nor had I ever been particularly obedient. I hate most authority figures, really, and defer to them reluctantly. But this new job didn't demand a lot of complex decision making, so it was a little easier to let go of the reins. Here, managers would be just as responsible for our failures or successes as we, and graded accordingly. In journalism, you wake up every single day—if you're any good or have any ambition—terrified you'll get something wrong and/or get beaten on a story by your many determined competitors. Your peers, in and outside of your workplace, can be scathing if you do. When you fail, it tends to be public and lonely.

In retail, working on the lowest rung of this large multinational organization was more of a team sport. We'd each bring our individual skills
and personality to the game, but specific losses—such as disappointing
in-store sales—wouldn't be, couldn't be, the fault of only one person. I
didn't design the clothes or shoot the photos for the posters. My coworkers were only there to sell: Tameisha didn't choose the color scheme for
the carpet, nor write the company's ad copy. None of us had decided we
should stock only red boys' ski jackets or those hideous pink scarves. We
were merely small moving parts in a much larger machine.

But how *would* it feel to serve? Many journalists enjoy considerable
autonomy, even envy or prestige, with professional access granted to
everyone from the President to celebrities. We don't consider ourselves
working-class.

I didn't mind the idea of serving, for a few reasons. I was older, perhaps a little wiser than if I'd tried this in my teens or twenties. Then, I
was impatient to rise in my chosen career. Now I was grateful for a break
from solitude and eager to polish my sales skills. I'd already achieved
enough success in my chosen field that a part-time, low-status job I considered temporary wouldn't exclusively define me. I'd been with my partner for ten years, had friends, my health, some retirement savings. The
rest of my life was pretty good.

Could it really hurt me to sell T-shirts for a while?

I reframed the notion of serving because, like many people, I don't
much like the word. Americans pride themselves on an egalitarian society premised on social mobility, not, as in some other cultures, on a
permanent servant class. I wasn't wild about being someone's serv*ant* or
being serv*ile*, but I do love *helping* people. I frequently stop lost tourists in
Manhattan to offer them assistance. I open doors and give up bus or sub-
way seats. I've mentored many other writers and enjoyed watching their
success. It's gratifying to ease someone's day, certainly when it only takes
a few minutes. Life is complicated enough that the simple idea of making
someone happy quickly seemed appealing indeed.

I'd be very happy to *help*.

The new job also put every aspect of our work habits and personalities under tremendous, relentless scrutiny. Instead of working by phone and chatting up sources, some of whom I'd never met face-to-face and never would, working retail demanded hours of face-to-face interaction, no matter what my mood or energy level that day. It isn't simply working *with* the public but done *in* public, from the minute you enter the store to the minute you clock out for break or at the end of a shift.

No longer, as I had for years with some editors on freelance projects, would I be able to work only through the emotionally opaque medium of e-mail. Now my demeanor and facial expressions, my hair and makeup, my perfume and accessories, my clothing, and my speed and tenor of response to even the stupidest questions or rudest comments were all visible and audible, recorded by multiple cameras and subject to formal review and a permanent record of written criticism.

I had made sure to tell Joe, during my job interview, that I enjoy getting along with a wide range of people of all ages and backgrounds. Which was, in fact, true. It's a basic skill for surviving in, let alone enjoying, journalism. You meet or interview all kinds, from cocky politicians to shy college students, new immigrants speaking broken English to CEOs. I lived for that mix. As one of my former *Daily News* colleagues said, "I love being surrounded all the time by strangers."

Joe had clearly decided to take a chance on me—someone with no retail experience, older, and clearly overqualified for the job, someone many others might have passed over or never even interviewed. They'd have assumed I would quit early on or I didn't have the physical stamina for long shifts or I'd talk down to my much younger coworkers or they wouldn't get along with me. None of which proved to be true.

I'd previously applied one Christmas to work part-time in the same mall at Nordstrom, a high-end department store that prides itself on excellent customer service. They wouldn't even interview me, but sat me down—as many retail employers now do to save time and money—at a computer, where I answered a long quiz designed to find out if I'd make a great saleswoman. Clearly not, since I never heard back from them.

Within weeks of starting at The North Face, I became the top-selling part-timer at our store, which consistently ranked in the top five, even three, of thirty stores nationwide. I sometimes sold more in my seven-hour shift than full-time employees did during their forty-hour workweek. It was not unusual, given a daily sales goal of $1,000, sometimes much more, for me to double or triple it.

Joe said he'd hired me for three reasons.

I was, in industry parlance, an "end-user," not just someone who could memorize all the features and benefits of the company's outdoor products but who could, as someone who uses this sort of gear, also extol the virtues of a waterproof shell for hiking New Zealand (been there) or a collapsible pack for traveling on a Eurail pass through Europe (did that) or even advise people on the weather or necessary vaccinations heading to East Africa (been there, too). I was an active athlete—a skier, skater, sailor, canoeist, hiker, camper, and walker—so could speak knowledge-ably and authoritatively about the value of one product over another.

I was also, he later told me, engaging, someone who, he saw at once in our interview, really enjoys initiating a conversation. I give him credit for that, for being so warm himself when we first met. Thanks to his candor and sincerity, I immediately liked him and wanted to work with him. I hadn't expected someone like him at all, having feared instead some robotic corporate warrior in a white shirt and striped tie, using "impact" as a verb. If Joe was someone who liked working for The North Face, and I liked and respected him after even one meeting, trying retail, even at this lowest level, seemed worth a shot.

Had he been as ferocious as some of the editors who'd interviewed me for journalism jobs, I'd probably have blown it, as I'd done before. It's embarrassing and a professional liability, but I respond very poorly when verbally attacked. I get defensive or go silent, no matter how badly I want the job, and end up looking passive and weak. One editor at *Portfolio*, then the hot new Condé Nast business magazine, told me he'd have thrown my clips in the garbage had they come in over the transom instead of thanks to my introduction from someone who'd hired him into a great job. What exactly *was* the point of being so insulting? I failed to offer a quick, witty rejoinder.

But I knew, and Joe quickly saw, that I brought transferable skills, no matter my personal sensitivities. Having met or interviewed everyone from the Queen of England to convicted felons meant I was comfortable in a wide range of situations, able to put almost anyone quickly at ease.

And, he admitted candidly—his consistently frank manner one of the reasons I liked him personally and liked working for him—they were simply desperate for staff. I was okay with that. He had grown up in an upper-middle-class family and knew, as I did after living in the county for twenty years, he'd never get the workers he *really* wanted: avid, skilled, passionate climbers and backpackers and hard-core adventurers; middle-class kids, or beyond, with terrific social and verbal skills who could easily relate to our affluent customers. For one thing, local kids are too busy cramming for SATs and burnishing their résumés so they can get into the Ivies. If they're mountain-climbing, it's in the Alps or Kilimanjaro so they've got something cool to boast about in their college essays, not the boring local Gunks, just up the Hudson River. They're not going to work part-time, most of them, because they don't need the money. And they, and their parents, certainly don't want anything as low-status as a retail sales job on their résumé. A prestigious, even unpaid Wall Street or Madison Avenue internship, sure.

When it came to hiring staff for the store, then, Joe pretty much had to take what he could get in the summer of 2007, long before the recession was even a dark cloud on the horizon. The recession really hit a year later and by December 2009 he could have had his pick of desperate workers—by then, nationally, there were six people applying for any job opening.

Not in 2007.

So the applicants Joe got, and those he hired, were almost all black and Hispanic men and women in their twenties and thirties of varying skills, education, intelligence and job history. For most of my tenure, two years and three months, I was our store's only long-term white female employee; only one other female Caucasian, a college student I never met, worked there part-time, and only for a few months. My coworkers mostly ranged in age from eighteen to thirty-four; Joe, at forty-five, was the second-oldest. Many were college-educated, some still in school, some with associate's degrees, a few of us with BAs. Four were parents, two with four children.

One of our associates, Tameisha, who had already been working full-time in retail for a decade, was so laconic she was practically mute with customers, but she was really smart, a quick study, and meticulous. Others were garrulous but bone-lazy, charming but never cleaned up, or diligent at folding and sensoring garments but much less adept at closing a sale. Another associate, Carol, and I got off to a terrible start, from which we never recovered. When we first met, I made a joke my coworkers knew was in jest but which she took to heart and held against me from then on. Even with others, Carol was a tough, mouthy little thing. Yet she managed to sell a lot of merchandise, so she must have poured on the charm to her customers.

A few of those who worked in our store were rumored to have felony convictions, I later discovered. I was shocked, although maybe I shouldn't have been. It was highly unlikely in any of my journalism jobs that anyone in the building, certainly at the bigger places, carried a criminal record. Sure, David Carr, *The New York Times*'s gravel-voiced media columnist, had written a bestselling memoir about his drug addiction and run-ins with the law. He was one in a million, lucky and talented enough to escape that past, snag a well-paid job, and later even safely capitalize on it.

I didn't know how to feel about working with colleagues who may have broken the law. At first it freaked me out. I don't even know what distinguishes a felony from a misdemeanor. Were these coworkers thieves?

Violent? Had they committed assault? Stolen a car? Sold drugs? It's not a question you can ask someone in casual conversation, even in private. I never did ask, and I never found out.

* * *

I couldn't imagine many associates who offered all the skills anyone really needed in this job. There are too many and they're often contradictory: extraordinary patience, unyielding tenacity, the ability to depersonalize endless rudeness and abuse, the emotional intelligence to connect well with a wide range of customers, a sense of humor, tact and diplomacy, unflappable calm, the ability to memorize reams of product data, uncomplaining submission to rigid corporate rules, the ability to work autonomously with little direct supervision, high energy and charm, attentive listening skills, the ability to be an astute (but discreet) observer, the ability to sell.

So, who *were* my new coworkers?

There were, in addition to the manager, Joe, and his assistant, Angela, only three full-timers. Most of us worked one to three shifts per week, typically fixed, so we could plan around them. I was the only Caucasian, the eldest, the only foreigner. Most had worked in retail before.

Few were especially outgoing, which made me wonder how well they would be able to sell. Journalists can usually chat up anyone, but even I found few points of entry with some of our coworkers, so little in common did we have. A few seemed extremely immature, but they were in their early twenties. How much could one expect?

One, Janelle, was a college student, her hooting laugh exploding at regular intervals. Tall and lean, she wore black velour sweatpants that clung to her every curve. Shenae, another college student, spent much of her time at work giggling, singing, and dancing.

Jorge, thirty-three, was lean and muscular, with broad shoulders and laughing black eyes. Flirtatious and teasing, he laughed easily, one of the few who could always get straitlaced Tameisha to crack a smile. He'd worked on a loading dock before this job, clearly relieved to leave behind more physical, less social tasks. With two daughters already, by two women living in different states, Jorge wasn't slowing down; I once took two phone calls at the store for him from two different women within seconds.

Bill, whose last job was in a supermarket meat department, was a quiet man of few words. With four young kids to keep track of, he spent much of his time phoning or texting them. On his break, he sat on a stool in the break area watching a DVD, listening to music on his iPhone, or fast asleep, his head planted on the Formica countertop.

Jared, twenty-three, chatty, and playful, had joined the National Guard—then bailed when he realized he'd be sent overseas to fight. "I didn't sign up for that!" he said. A slight man with pale skin, he seemed unbothered by almost anything, his optimism often a breath of needed helium on our grimmest days. An avid outdoorsman (unlike many of our associates), he dreamed of attending the Harvard of outdoor training, the National Outdoor Leadership School.

Our manager, Joe, defied my every cliché of a military veteran: soft-spoken, funny, down-to-earth, warm. He'd worked in retail for more than a decade, ever since leaving the service, for major companies like Pottery Barn and Bed Bath & Beyond. Short and powerfully built, Joe, like me, lived to travel.

Angie, his assistant, reminded me of a rabbit—shy and gentle, her voice barely above a whisper, who, when upset or embarrassed, flushed deeply. A lifelong Bronx resident, Puerto Rican in origin, by twenty-six, she'd worked for several smaller retailers. Coming to The North Face was a big step up. While our store was being built, she met and fell in love with Sam, a carpenter on the project. Within a year, they'd moved in together. A year later, unmarried, they had a baby.

I wondered how we'd all get along. Since graduating from the University of Toronto in 1979, I had only worked within my chosen field, whether for newspapers, television, magazines, or wire services. My managers and coworkers, in Montreal, Paris, or small-town New Hampshire, were all college-educated, some with master's degrees, even a few with PhDs, MBAs, or law or medical degrees. That mattered to me. Not their degrees or their pedigrees per se, but knowing that most colleagues, having survived the brutal weeding-out it typically took to win a decently paid journalism job, brought a standard package of skills, aptitudes, and attitude: intelligence, cultural or political sophistication, avid curiosity, and, often, a deep, driving ambition.

I had always wanted to work with the very best whenever possible; like them, wanting to get ahead, to rise—and, always, with a deep shared satisfaction, to kick our competitors' asses.

But these expectations were normal in a world of Ivy League degrees and polite locutions, people who avidly read—and wrote for—the most exclusive media outlets, like *The New York Times*, *The Atlantic*, or *The New Yorker*. People who summer, using the noun as a verb, in elite enclaves like Nantucket or Easthampton.

I'd never spent time, socially or professionally, with anyone who had a visible tattoo, or several, who traded the names of their favorite ink artists the way my friends mentioned that of a chic Kensington hotel or a great West Village colorist. I knew only one person who'd grown up poor, in New York City public housing, now a lawyer. No one I knew lived in public housing or had no fixed address, as several of my new coworkers did, couch-surfing from one relative or friend's home to another.

From the very start, I heard persistent rumors about several of our employees using drugs, smoking pot on the job. I didn't care. I hate infighting, so whenever someone told me this, and I would hear it repeatedly over the years I worked there, I shrugged and shut the gossiper down. I don't do drugs and cared only that our team was hardworking and friendly. My life had been full of unwanted drama at the *Daily News*. The whole point of this job was to escape that.

But it was clear I'd need to rethink my values if I was going to survive, let alone thrive, within retail. I'd have to reexamine whatever comforting assumptions I'd held for decades about what makes a worker valuable or a friend appealing. I'd never known anyone like my new coworkers. Two, in their early thirties, each already had four young children; journalism's unpredictable hours meant that many of my former colleagues postponed or never had kids, and certainly did not have more than one or two. I'd never known a single mother who hadn't made the choice to bear and raise a child alone unless after much deliberation, and only with a steady, healthy professional income.

Until now, no one I knew lived in the neighborhoods my new coworkers inhabited: Yonkers, Mount Vernon, Washington Heights, Harlem, and the Bronx. I'd never worked with a war veteran, let alone one who had served in the Special Forces, and knew only two who had served, both in the Navy. I didn't know any avid outdoorsmen like my new boss, Joe. Journalists, often too broke or tired to do much in their leisure hours, now looked pretty boring in comparison.

The black and Hispanic journalists I knew who'd managed to claw their way into well-paid or prestigious journalism jobs were, by necessity if not by their natures, safely corporate and deracinated, soft-spoken and polite in silk and linen and Brooks Brothers. My new coworkers wore do-rags and had multiple tattoos and piercings and long, wildly decorated fingernails. One young woman, Andrea, had a mini-constellation circling the nape of her neck, three blue stars, in outline, of different sizes. She was a light-skinned Hispanic in her early twenties, and, as the French say, *bien dans sa peau*—comfortable in her own skin. I admired Andrea's confidence. I liked being around people tattooed and pierced, happy to simply be themselves. Now, maybe I could be as well. To win respect or acceptance in the store, under the hot spotlights and security cameras' gaze, I didn't have to make front page or have a new book coming out from a major publisher or drive thousands of visitors to my blog.

I just had to show up, work well, get along with everyone, and go home. The pressure I'd always felt since college, to achieve, to win, to beat others, to make my name, was off for now.

I liked that simplicity. I was ready for a little simple.

But would the staff of our store even *like* one another? Would we share jokes? What would we talk about?

Who would turn out to be the laziest—or the most hardworking? Who, if anyone, would be fired? Or promoted? How long, given the brief tenure of retail, would any of us even last?

* * *

Our newly assembled team, typical in some ways, was highly unusual in others. We had received four full days of training. *Paid* training. We had been interviewed face-to-face, not by a computer quiz. The North Face had treated all of us to a good meal in a nice hotel, giving us a chance to get to know one another socially, even if briefly, away from the sales floor and stockrooms. We were given new, attractive, comfortable clothing and footwear as our uniform.

Industry experts I spoke with all confirmed how poorly and haphazardly many—if not most—retailers still hire. Few train their staff. They gamble (with 100 percent turnover each year an accepted, hidden, and unchallenged cost of doing business) that they're just wasting their time and money on employees who will leave for something better, and better paid, as soon as they can find it. The fact most *don't* train, while pressuring employees to sell 30 percent APR store credit cards, clean the toilets, and answer sometimes extremely challenging questions demanding extensive product knowledge, does increase the odds of that annual exodus.

Many frustrated associates told me they hated knowing so little about their jobs, tossed onto the sales floor of even well-known stores like Williams-Sonoma and J.Crew with little or no preparation to face customers' reasonable expectations that they actually knew something. Shoppers' equal frustration with their incompetence was predictable, demoralizing—and fairly inevitable.

Mel Kleiman, director of Humetrics, a company that helps retailers find and retain associates, was stunned when I told him we had received twenty-four hours of paid training—something so rare only 10 percent of associates get it, he said.

Even then, several of our associates bailed within months. Darla, a young woman, gratefully left for a telemarketing job paying $15 an hour, $6 an hour more than The North Face had offered her. She wouldn't have to stand on her feet for hours, deal with people face-to-face, or wear a uniform. Let alone pay for parking.

Who could blame her? Yet the company also thereby lost some of our best salespeople. Even though she was barely out of college, Darla was a pro I turned to in desperation whenever a customer had frayed my last nerve. Nothing fazed her, and I was awed by her ability to stay cool, calm, and good-humored.

Part of why Americans often tolerate such terrible service as customers, and give it as associates, is a widespread, long-standing gentlemen's agreement: I'm not paying very much for this reduced-price or heavily discounted T-shirt/sofa/television set, so I don't *really* expect you to be helpful or knowledgeable. I just want the lowest prices possible.

Only at the very highest levels—at costly department stores like Neiman Marcus or Nordstrom, or a luxury retailer like Tiffany or Hermès or Gucci—is this model abandoned. (A lifetime shopper at Holt Renfrew, Canada's most exclusive department store chain, I had no idea there was a separate, private entrance in an anonymous office building next door to their store on Bloor Street, Toronto's equivalent of upper Madison or Rodeo Drive. It's reserved for their best customers, explained industry expert Paco Underhill, those who spend in a month what some of us earn annually.) "The most important customer in any store is the one you'll never see on the [sales] floor," he says, although I did once see actress

Keira Knightley in the tiny-but-fabulous accessories department of that Holt's location. Harrods, the 162-year-old London emporium that draws fifteen million customers every year, even offers a helicopter-and-aircraft charter service.

At that price point, when associates are likely earning a healthy 6 to 8 percent commission on each sale, plus possible bonuses and a higher hourly wage or salary, wealthy customers have their own vendeuse, someone who knows their size(s) and taste, their social and philanthropic and professional commitments, the climates and locations of their multiple homes.

One American company exemplifies this, comprising the San Francisco institution Wilkes Bashford (named for its previous owner), with a second store in Palo Alto and Mitchells in Westport, Richards in Greenwich, and Marshs in Huntington, Long Island. The stores serve some of the nation's wealthiest customers. All are owned by the genial, bestselling author of two business books, *Hug Your Customers* and *Hug Your People*, Jack Mitchell. He's a legend in the industry, yet, unusual for an executive at his level, didn't insist on having a PR person oversee our interview or demand to see my questions in advance. Instead, in his typically modest fashion, he only told me after our hour-long meeting he'd been asked to address his peers 214 times in six years.

I met him on a rainy gray morning in March, when he bounded down the wide white marble staircase of his Greenwich, Connecticut, store, a cloth tape measure draped around his neck. His eyes met mine. His smile was warm and he shook my hand before politely asking if I could wait a minute. He walked over to join a young male sales associate helping a slim, white-haired, distinguished-looking gentleman into a cream linen blazer. The conversation between the three was low-key, gently bantering, and affectionate as they assured him—one of the most powerful men on Wall Street—the jacket looked terrific and fit him well.

The airy store, twenty-five thousand square feet, is flooded with indirect natural light from its high clerestory windows on even an overcast day. Its affluent customers, accustomed to white-glove service, know they can call associates and managers at home, at night, on the weekends; they'll even rush to the airport or to a client's office or home to make sure the tux/gown/sports coat/suede lace-ups are delivered exactly when they're needed.

That attentiveness is modeled and expected at Mitchell's from an associate's very first day. Jack Mitchell and his team hires *very* carefully, and only then after as many as eight personal interviews with members of his staff.

"It does come from the top," says Mitchell. "It comes from the owners, the managers, the leaders of the business. They have to be positive, passionate, and personal." Even after decades serving others, Mitchell radiates pleasure in his work—and deplores the terrible customer service many of us have simply come to accept. He'd recently read a profile of the CEO of Sears: "Not once did they talk about customer service! Life could be so much easier and better for [associates]," he argued. "You have to say, 'Good morning!' I think it's very possible to treat associates well. You just have to decide you want to do it."

Being kind and respectful to workers—never calling them, for example, "the help" or even "employees"—sends a clear and powerful message, he said. It also produces clear, measurable bottom-line results: "They can be much more productive!"

"Our retail systems are based on a lower-middle-class functionality," agrees Paco Underhill, whose firm Envirosell is hired by major retailers worldwide to help them better understand their customers' behavior and increase profits by selling to them most effectively.

"Service in the U.S. is almost always *friendly*," he says. "But how *professional* is it?"

He contrasts retailers' and shoppers' sharply curbed expectations stateside with those in France, Germany, and other European nations. "There, there's a tradition of selling to the aristocracy that goes back five hundred years. Selling for a living, in Europe, has therefore over time acquired an air of middle-class respectability. The role of the associate has been institutionalized, as to what an associate *is*. They're often an adult, even middle-aged, and frequently a union member. In Europe, it's usually someone's full-time job. You very rarely see part-time help." This is in contrast to American retail, where 34 percent of the retail associates are part-timers, often poorly paid and without benefits. "In Europe, the view is: 'This is my job. I take pride in my job. It's reasonably well paid and so I take pride in it.' The nature of the service culture is historically very different here in the U.S. than it is anywhere else.

"In the U.S.," Underhill continues, "almost every American kid, regardless of social status, will probably work retail for a while when they're in their teens or early twenties. In Italy, France, and Germany, partly because of legal restrictions on teen employees, kids have *no* experience working."

When a customer in Des Moines or Detroit or Santa Barbara, then, sees an unpolished or inexperienced young adult giving lousy service, he or she is more willing to shrug it off "because this could be one of my own kids," Underhill explains.

So, for many Americans, a stint behind the cash wrap is a rite of passage, something you do for a little while, a few months or a summer or over the holidays, probably blowing much of your paycheck—depending on your circumstances—on the (likely steeply employee-discounted) merchandise sold by your employer. I saw this at our store with two employees in particular, both young men from well-off families, who were clearly most interested in how much loot they could scoop up and show off to their friends. Even my colleagues with children bought a lot for themselves and their families, happy to have access to a coveted and well-known brand more affordably.

Still, the word industry veterans most often used, and casually, to describe retail associates? Disposable.

"We don't *look* to rise in retail," says Underhill. "They are hiring associates with the express idea they're traded in and out. Their time span is limited. It's *meant* to be a part-time job and the retail associate's position isn't perceived as a career. The American model of business doesn't allow for it."

This attitude isn't new, writes Ellen Ruppel Shell in her book *Cheap*, but began more than a century ago with Frank Winfield Woolworth and Sebastian Sperling Kresge, America's first cut-price merchants. "Woolworth only hired the cheapest labor to serve on the store floor, and most of that time that meant young, unmarried women. In the chain's early years, he paid these clerks two or three dollars a week, not a living wage even then . . . it was part of his plan . . . 'One thing is certain [he wrote in a memo to his managers]: we cannot afford to pay good wages and sell goods as we do now, *and our clerks ought to know it*'" [italics mine].

Most of Woolworth's employees were low-skilled and poorly paid cashiers. In 1892, then, these two industry leaders of American retail made the point as clear as the Walmarts and Dollar Stores do today—that working on the sales floor isn't a valuable skill worth a living wage.

According to Underhill, the logic is simple: it costs money to hire, train, and fully staff stores. Those able to function with the fewest bodies (and the more part-timers without benefits or paid vacation or sick days, the better), working the fewest hours, win. Lower costs equal higher profits.

"The only factor you can control is the cost of labor. The landlord? The heat? You can't control those costs." This puts hiring managers under "tremendous pressure to control labor costs," he says.

The inevitable result? "The level of service in many American stores is not too hot," he admits.

"Most companies are not customer-centric," agrees Milton Pedraza, CEO of the Luxury Institute, a six-year-old Manhattan-based independent research and consulting firm that helps the highest-end companies, from Tiffany to Ritz-Carlton to Gucci and HSBC, figure out how to attract and nurture the nation's most affluent consumers. The institute defines these as shoppers with an average household income of $845,000 and assets of $16.6 million.

"Retailers remain channel-centric—'We're a hotel'—or product-centric—'We sell shoes or handbags,'" he says. "They focus on, 'This is what we make and sell.' Or they are store-centric. They talk a lot about service, but they don't really execute." Pedraza dismisses "the talent myth."

"What you need instead is a self-reinforcing system. You have to have the right service values, the right service standards, the right people, the right education, the right incentives and daily rituals. You have to constantly measure the customer experience to make sure the service values are being lived by every single associate every day."

Too many retailers are still hiring people who just need a job, and retail sales require little formal and no specialized or graduate or professional education. Instead, retailers need to select and educate only those who intrinsically thrive on helping others, whose real source of joy is making others happy, Pedraza says. Truly giving service must drive these workers, he says.

Rare among his peers, he also advocates making retail sales a job truly worth keeping. "Retailers need to nurture and care for their associates as much as they do for their customers. Retailers need to create great incentives including fair wages, bonuses, and recognition programs that reward those who live the values and make clients feel special while achieving sales results."

"The industry in general needs to hire people who *really* want to be in retail," he says. But, instead, too many in this industry cheap out, preferring to pay rock-bottom wages. And the hiring managers, under intense pressure from their distant corporate head offices to save money, themselves C-suite executives with Wall Street analysts breathing down their necks demanding healthy profits and steady growth, scrimp where they can, and where they must. At the cash wrap.

It's the only wiggle room they have left—because it's all the company has left them. The store premises have a lease or purchase price long ago negotiated and agreed to, and commercial rents can and do sky-rocket without warning. The merchandise was long ago chosen, ordered, shipped, distributed, marketed, and advertised. Every possible cost has already been assumed. Now, thanks to decades if not centuries of received wisdom—"That's just retail"—there's only one place left to save: *paying your frontline employees the least the local market will bear.*

Many store managers are already under the gun to follow company-wide marching orders from head office, complete with corporate-issued templates and graphs. Hiring their own staff their way may be one of very few activities left to them that allows for personal preference or auton-omy. This, says Pedraza, is unwise, as managers still rely too heavily on their own personal impressions when hiring, not on the more objective, time-tested psychological measurements he feels much more accurately predict who will shine as a salesperson and who's just a chatty, charming interview.

"They hire the wrong people," says Pedraza. "Not everyone gets a high from serving people, and you need only people who *love* to take care of other people." Using these tests, as mass retailers like Walmart do to quickly weed through thousands of applicants, offers retailers a better shot at hiring the person with the right aptitudes, he insists. "You have to give yourself a higher percentage for possible success, and to do this you need better data from which to make decisions."

What do psychological tests used for hiring, often a series of ques-tions designed to sniff out the unsuitable, actually prove? "Whether you're an optimist or a pessimist," for example. "If you're an optimist, you can handle rejection. It will show if you're *really* customer-centric."

I wondered if Joe would have hired me—or many of us—if I'd had to take such tests. I bet he never even would have *met* me. I would have been tidily and metrically rebuffed. Surely the tests would have quickly detected my short fuse and low tolerance for snobs. Nor am I wild about poorly behaved small children, and I *really* hate people who snap their fingers at me. But would these tests also have discovered my warmth and teasing, playful sense of humor, my fluent French and Spanish? How about my strong work ethic or my collegiality or my experience playing more than a dozen sports and visiting thirty-seven countries?

* * *

One of the challenges of managing a retail operation is finding willing victims, aka sales associates. It's different at high-end stores where wealthy customers, excellent sales skills, high-end goods, and solid commissions can make the job worth wanting and keeping, an enjoyable career spanning years, perhaps decades. I heard from a former associate there that Bergdorf Goodman, the costly and exclusive Manhattan department store, was in 2009 paying some associates $25 an hour; one of my customers who once worked there said she made tremendous money on her commissions and urged me to apply. Perhaps selling luxury goods to discerning customers—not harried housewives in a hurry, as we often did—is a wholly different experience than the kind of work we were doing. I realized very quickly a higher-end store wouldn't necessarily be a better fit for me; I'm not a cooing fashionista, or a size 4, and basically loathe rich snobs. The percentage of those would be much higher in a store catering primarily to the wealthy. Better to keep my sales high and my blood pressure manageable, even for a lower income.

Anyone charged with hiring and managing poorly paid workers who won't ever receive significant raises or commissions, no matter their skill or hard work, and whose odds of moving up the ladder into management are slim to none, faces a tough job. If our store's staffers had better vocational choices, they would have already made them. Or perhaps they'd already given up on work as their primary source of pride and pleasure, still a fairly standard expectation of many white-collar workers. There remains a significant disconnect between what all of us most want, retailers and customers alike—great service and well-trained staff—and the reality on the sales floor. Well-compensated corporate managers, and even store managers, see retail as their career, not just a job. They reasonably want and need lower level workers who share their strong work ethic and sense of professional pride. But they expect all this from workers whom they pay badly and often treat badly.

Associates, no matter how young or poorly educated or lacking better job offers, aren't fools.

And so many of my coworkers, even in their early to mid-twenties, were less driven by meeting The North Face's arbitrary and ever-changing sales targets than by achieving their own personal goals, whether having another child, finishing school, or saving up to travel. There was a serious and unresolvable difference, then, between what our corporate managers routinely expected of us, sitting multiple time zones distant from the sales floors, and what their younger, poorly paid associates were willing or able to provide them.

You get what you pay for.

Unless you're extremely determined to rise into management, and hope to do so quickly, working as a retail associate—no matter how fancy or costly the merchandise you're moving—quickly becomes just another job, and one with extremely limited intellectual challenges and severely restricted wages. Some of my colleagues had been fired from a few positions or had a lousy work ethic. Some certainly lacked ambition, but this work also offered us no incentive to excellence, short of simply keeping our poorly paid jobs.

The associates who were said to have criminal records, as one of them told me, found getting *any* job difficult. (They were all consistently collegial and hard-working.) When people can only negotiate bottom-of-the-barrel fees for their labor, they're either settling for whatever they can get quickly and easily—or just can't get anything better.

From the start, I was consistently impressed by Joe and Angie's calm, low-key management style. They weren't sloppy or inattentive, but their manner, in marked contrast to the rigidity of the parent company employing all of us, was largely and blessedly hands-off. We all knew what was expected of us, but rarely, in my case at least, were we reminded of it. Unlike, say, Walmart, which expects its employees to start each day with a group cheer, there was little company-enforced regimentation of how and when we were to do our jobs. Joe and Angela treated most of us with the logical, adult assumption that we knew what to do and how to figure things out. However, they fired several slackers, three for lousy work habits and one for theft. It didn't happen quickly, and they seemed willing to do whatever they could to retain staff. But there was a breaking point and we all knew it.

That sent a clear message to the rest of us.

And any retail manager knows the statistic, or should: *50 percent of retail associates,* a figure I viscerally now appreciate, are gone from their jobs within ninety days. *Three months.* They quit or they're fired. Industry turnover remains a shocking—and largely shrugged-off—100 percent a year.

Employees quit, my coworkers and others working elsewhere have told me, because:

- It was boring. They simply couldn't take the tedium.
- Their coworkers, fighting for commissions, were sharks.
- Their feet and legs hurt from so much standing and walking.
- They were saddled, in addition to sales duties, with additional unpaid work like security and cleaning the store, even the bathrooms.
- The money was lousy and never got any better.
- The long hours, weekend work, back-to-back shifts. Late closings, early openings, not to mention overnight or split shifts and constantly changing schedules, made family life or other commitments difficult.

- They disliked the rigidity with which the company conducted its business, such as requiring employees to use scripts or push high-interest store credit cards.
- Customers were rude and demanding.

No wonder—even as the Bureau of Labor projects an 8 percent rise in the number of retail associate positions between now and 2018, an additional 374,700 positions—few people really want to end up in one.

Too bad, then, that retail is the fastest-growing source of new American jobs.

FOUR

HOLIDAY SHOPPING BEGINS:
DECK THE HALLS, NOT THE CUSTOMERS!

A new sales supervisor, Peter, joined our staff in November of 2007, soon after we opened. A large, tall, tattooed man whose age was hard to peg—I guessed thirty-two or so—he carried himself stiffly and officiously. He was, in this respect, noticeably different from the rest of us. Why was someone so unfriendly working in a job that requires great people skills?

A retail manager, even after thoughtfully assembling a hardworking team, needs sensitivity to handle a group that might include high school grads and graduate students working together. No matter how serious the work, retail associates *need* a light touch because retail itself is just so hard, both physically and emotionally. Add to these grueling demands the corporate ethics codes and behavioral standards, uniforms and dress codes and handbooks bristling with rules and regulations and manuals of an almost military rigidity—and a martinet is quickly resented, disobeyed, or ignored whenever possible.

Oddly, Peter didn't seem to care what effect his prickliness had on the rest of us. I wondered how things might change with his arrival, and feared the worst. Joe, our store manager, was easygoing and friendly, not one to stand on ceremony, as Peter seemed determined to do. I wondered what Joe saw in him.

Peter's haughty demeanor soon prompted an angry confrontation.

"You never say hello to us! We say hello to you, but you never answer. What's up with that?" demanded Shaniqua during our monthly meeting. We didn't care if he was our new supervisor. We were used to, and valued, a warmer, more collegial style. Training for and opening a brand-new store together had built us into a team. Peter, even if he had new authority over us, was now the not-very-welcome newcomer. Didn't he realize he needed to make even a token effort?

"I have a hearing problem," he replied. "It isn't deliberate. I just don't hear everything people say to me."

No one bought it. He was perfectly able to initiate a greeting, saying, "Hey!" to us as consistently and cheerfully as Angie or Joe did, and we all knew it.

We'd already fallen into a groove. We basically liked one another and, despite some sniping and gossip, got along well for a group whose ages ranged from eighteen to fifty, and which included college students, ex-soldiers, and parents of small children. One good thing, maybe the only good thing, about working without commission was that it leveled the playing field. While some people stole sales—entering their six-digit employee number at the cash wrap instead of that of the person on the floor who'd actually done the work to make the sale—the stakes were low enough that we were all equally screwed. It created its own sad solidarity.

Thankfully, even after Peter's arrival, no one stood over us, telling us what to do. A sheet printed out daily designated which of the store's three zones we'd be working that day, which cash register to use, and our daily sales goal, a number that was always changing. Those daily goals felt like a weird game to me, some sort of corporate eight ball, as almost every day was different. The goals were never discussed or explained, not to me anyway, and never in our monthly meetings. Where did they come from? Why were they so high one day and so much lower the next?

It quickly became clear that having or showing any strong curiosity about these sales goals, and why they changed and who was setting them and how we were doing compared to other North Face stores or others in our industry, was . . . a little strange. No one but me ever seemed to care. My caring made me stand out, and not in a good way. It was clear we were hired hands, not expected or meant to invest much energy or interest in the company's success. They didn't care if we were interested. If anyone in management wanted our opinions, and clearly they didn't, they'd have asked us for them.

I'd asked repeatedly in training, what if we fell short and didn't meet a sales goal? We'd be coached, they said, but no one would be fired for not meeting the goals.

Angela, our assistant manager, was still feeling her way. At twenty-five, she wasn't much older than many of the girls she supervised and we could sense her nervousness. She had plenty of retail experience, but only at smaller stores, and it was clear she felt somewhat out of her depth. She was also the only female manager; Joe, Peter, and Mark (now gone) were all male and older. And Joe and Peter were avid outdoorsmen, which they loved to talk about for hours. Angie was not.

I remembered my own anxiety when I taught undergraduate journalism students, some only five or six years my junior, in Montreal. In my nervousness and inexperience, I was a hard-ass, brandishing my new authority partly out of my own insecurity. When I saw Angela doing the same thing to us, I tried to remember that desire to prove yourself in a new job managing others.

But it was tough at first.

One day, standing in front of my locker—located behind closed doors and off the sales floor away from customers—I grabbed a quick bite of apple. I usually worked from one p.m. until six p.m. with no break, went for my meal, and worked again until closing. We never got any other breaks. I was often ravenous by four or five and I needed a hit of energy; we weren't allowed to eat or drink anywhere near the sales floor. The stockrooms or the bathroom were our only options for privacy away from those security cameras and customers' or "secret shoppers'" possible disapproval.

But even that narrow, crowded, hidden hallway offered no real respite from observation or criticism.

Angie was walking past the lockers when she saw me.

"Are you on your break?" she asked sarcastically. We both knew I wasn't.

I couldn't believe she cared that much. No customer could see me. I was taking perhaps thirty seconds away from my official duties. Why did this even *matter*?

I said nothing, but felt humiliated and small as she walked away, her point made. She never mentioned it again, but she didn't have to. She'd flexed her managerial muscle.

Peter's arrival created something of a seismic shift. We were suddenly on notice to be . . . *something* more, something quicker, something better. Why? Neither Angie nor Joe had shown displeasure with our performance. By now they knew our work styles and managed us accordingly. But here was Peter, frosty and monosyllabic, hired to oversee us when it wasn't clear to any of us that we *needed* overseeing. No one bothered to explain what he was there to do or why it needed doing. He'd been hired. That's all we needed to know.

By November, the Christmas season was in full swing. Boxes of new stock arrived almost daily, a Niagara of product. The bulky cardboard containers were piling up so quickly it was sometimes impossible to access the stockroom quickly or easily. That meant more time lost and wasted determining if we even *had* something in stock.

These boxes weren't labeled with their contents.

I couldn't believe it. The only way to know what was in one was to open it, especially if we needed something specific for a waiting customer that wasn't already out on the shelves. Every box warned NO BOX CUTTERS! in large letters. Right. How else could we open them, by the dozen, as fast as possible?

The North Face is owned by the VF Corporation, the world's largest apparel maker, an international manufacturer and distributor of multiple brands. If anyone, anywhere, in this industry had the resources and expertise to nail down the swift and efficient movement of their products, surely they had. Why didn't we have three or four or five stockroom clerks—as many as it took to make sure that all stock was easily and quickly available for the sales staff all the time? Because, as always, it was cheaper to use fewer staff. We did have stockroom clerks, but few, and only during the daytime.

Associates had no way to access the company's Web site. If we were out of stock, we had to call another store, ask a busy associate there to try and locate an item, wait on hold for many long minutes, and, if out of luck, start the whole process again with another busy store and another overworked associate. Our customers bristled with technology, using their BlackBerrys and cell phones to snap and transmit photos of our clothes to a friend or relative for approval. Often they preshopped on the Web and came in asking for something specific, unable to believe that a North Face store didn't carry every single item the company makes. Nor could we quickly and easily locate what they wanted and get it for them.

At Lord & Taylor's busy Manhattan shoe department, years earlier, sales associates were issued handheld devices telling them instantly what's in the back room, and alerting a clerk there to bring it to the floor. It's an impressive, smooth, time-saving win-win for customer and associate—customers can shop more comfortably (and feel less guilty asking for a dozen pairs at once), and the poor associates aren't wasting time, energy, and sales by schlepping back and forth with heavy boxes piled up to their chin. In 2010, Home Depot decided to spend $60 million to equip its associates with similar devices. Not us. Instead, we faced an unpredictable, unholy frenzy. And, when boxes started arriving almost hourly, it was suddenly all hands on deck: open, unpack, sort, sensor, and stack or hang it all. The remaining stock, heavy boxes, were then piled twenty feet above the stockroom floor—where none of us could easily reach them quickly.

Once each box was stored near the ceiling, a sheet of eight-by-ten paper listed its contents in thirty-six-point type so we could see at a glance if we even had a certain jacket or sweater. But we still didn't know how many of them each box contained or what sizes. If a stockroom clerk wasn't available to clamber up there like a monkey, wrangle a box, and toss down what we needed, too bad. And, most evenings, the stock clerks had gone home, leaving this problem for each of us sales associates to solve.

Half the time I just gave up looking for something, even though professional pride told me not to. I'd paw fruitlessly through half a dozen boxes, then, thoroughly pissed off at this amateurish chaos and wasted time, go back to the sales floor to disappoint yet another would-be buyer.

Like waiters with hungry customers who'd punish them for a slow-moving meal, our customers were quick to tongue-lash us if they felt inconvenienced. Even if it wasn't our fault. The gap between what demanding consumers expected of us and the tools allowing us to meet those expectations was much wider than—as a shopper, certainly—I could have imagined.

We needed more shepherd's hooks, the light, expanding aluminum poles needed to reach high-hanging clothing fast; brightly lit stockrooms offering visible, easy access to everything in them (or full-time staff to find it for us and bring it out to us); and clean, clear pathways and stockroom floors. Behind closed doors, far away from customers' gazes, unused mannequins or display stands often crowded the narrow hallways, their sharp steel arms protruding, creating an additional obstacle course.

Then, just in time for the holiday season, the busiest month of the retail year, I injured myself. While I was doing push-ups in my jazz dance class, my right shoulder made an ominous crunch. The orthopedic surgeon said I had an impingement, fancy talk for difficulty moving my right arm. Of course, I was right-handed—and now I couldn't raise my right arm above shoulder level. So much for stacking shelves and reaching to zip up jackets or even check a size tag on the higher racks.

I told Joe and Angela, who were sympathetic, and who agreed I could keep working. With only fifteen people on our staff, I assumed they'd tell Peter, our new, tough supervisor on the sales floor. But they didn't. One afternoon, in his typically charmless fashion, he barked a command at me to load one shelf and stack another. Bitchy from pain, tired from the stepped-up holiday pace, unaccustomed to so starchy a management style from someone who'd made no effort to get to know us, I answered rudely.

"*Simultaneously?*"

"I don't appreciate the banter," he sniffed.

"Banter? Banter? I don't banter, Peter."

"Enough with the backchat."

"Backchat?"

I'd never spoken so rudely to a supervisor. But neither had one spoken to me as he might a distracted three-year-old.

"Get off the floor. Now!" he barked, hustling me away from the customers—which even in my anger I knew was the right decision—and into the store's tiny office. It was barely five feet square.

"Go home," he said.

"Fine," I muttered.

I tore off my plastic name tag, jammed on my coat, and headed for the door.

"Where are you going?" asked Angela, who saw me leaving. "Your shift isn't over."

"I've just been fired," I told her.

"Fired? You haven't been fired. You've just been sent home, that's all."

Was this some sort of adult time-out? I had no idea.

"Let's go back to the office and sort this out," she said.

I'd been shouted at in several newsrooms in front of colleagues—as had many others over my years in journalism. No supervisor there had ever tried to calm things down or resolve a problem.

At the *Daily News*, my star, never high to begin with at a bare-knuckled tabloid, fell fast and hard after Michael Cooke, the editor-in-chief, a former colleague from Canada, left to return to the *Chicago Sun-Times*. Bill Harrison, my direct boss, stopped speaking to me. I asked him to go out for lunch, to get some idea what my future there now held.

"I don't take lunch," he replied.

"Then let's go out for coffee," I persisted. "We need to talk about my work here."

"When I want to talk to you, I'll let you know," he drawled.

Things went from bad to worse as I sat at my desk for seventeen days without an assignment. The paper's motto, I was told by thirty-year veterans and the head of human resources himself, was, "Sink or swim."

Still, I'd never cried at work. Not there, not anywhere.

That was about to change, to my shame and embarrassment.

Peter and I began shouting at each other so loudly that I thought the one glass wall of the office—a space so small, filled with a desk and computers and shelves and a fax machine, that it was hard for us not to touch one another—would shatter.

"I don't have to take this! I don't have to work retail!" he yelled.

I said the same thing.

Angela, her eyes widening, tried to mediate between a very large, very proud, and very angry black man and a somewhat smaller but equally angry and prideful white woman who was more than twice Angie's age and, it turned out, his as well.

God help her.

Quiet, meek Angela shouted us down. "Let him have his say. Let her speak!" she told us both sharply.

I lost it, finally weeping in frustration, exhaustion, and shame. I felt like I was working my ass off, in ways I'd never imagined. It was a crummy job, poorly paid. Why was I even bothering? And now I was getting my ass chewed by some jerk half my age?

I wouldn't quit. Not over this. I'm not a quitter. I'd just been hired two months earlier. And I needed the income.

No one ever said, "Thanks" or "Good job." The callousness was demoralizing, especially when my shoulder ached all day, every day, no matter what I did. Now I understood why 50 percent of retail workers are gone within ninety days, whether they have been fired or quit. It's just low-wage, thankless, repetitive work and the recompense minimal. (And yet, six of our original team of fifteen remained even more than two years later, highly unusual in retail, less unusual in the more stable niche of the outdoor clothing industry. Our managers did, eventually, learn to say, "Thank you.")

Peter finally apologized for being so rough. After the smoke cleared, it was obvious to all three of us that he and I were actually pretty similar, both hardheaded high achievers, both former competitive athletes, people who liked to stay in control and win. Too bad we had to learn this about each other the hard way, that we had a lot more in common than we'd realized. But at least now we knew.

I headed home for a badly needed nap, mortified at having become so emotional and losing my self-control. I was surprised I hadn't been fired on the spot for insubordination, and grateful that I hadn't. Even if this was hardly a dream job, it was a job I had trained hard to learn, was very new to, and still wanted to do well.

I hadn't had a job in a year. It felt like three. I wanted to do this one right.

I'd also learned a lot about young, quiet Angie. Few managers of any age could have handled and ultimately defused such a nasty confrontation. I appreciated her coolheaded skill in the face of so much raw emotion.

* * *

Every few weeks, the store got remade by Zeke, our merchandising guy. Tall and lean, wearing low-cut jeans that advertised his washboard abs and narrow hips, his glossy black hair slipping into his eyes, Zeke was a veritable rock star, a traveling guru who moved around the region redoing displays for all our stores and some of the many other retailers who sold our products.

The first thing you lose when working retail, like any job, really, is control over your environment, something that I had a complete fiat over when working from home. One reason we were so happy to see Zeke was the cool music he played through the store's speaker system from his iPod, a desperately needed break from the stunningly bad music inflicted on us by Muzak. Music was something I cared a lot about. Working alone at home meant tuning in to whatever I pleased; now, listening to dreck over and over for seven hours at a stretch was torture some days. I simply couldn't believe how horrible the store's music was—"Fly Like an Eagle"? If a supposedly cutting-edge store was playing faded 1970s-era music like this—compared to Anthropologie, whose music was quirky, quiet, and hip, a distinct echo of the vintage, unique, and mass-marketed merchandise itself—what subliminal message was this company sending? It was old-fart music, hardly sounds that would attract or appeal to today's customers.

Zeke had come to set up our holiday look, one that included tall, rectangular glass vases filled with silver ornaments and white wooden trees composed of spray-painted twigs. They were the most artificial natural things I'd ever seen. I could barely imagine the amount spent on their creation and distribution. Those little wooden trees with their fragile, spiky branches had come thickly wrapped in bubble wrap, smothered in Styrofoam peanuts, and shipped in thick cardboard boxes. The money wasted was mind-blowing; we threw out hundreds of plastic bags every time we opened a box of new merchandise. Where did it all go? Was any of it being recycled?

I cared less about where all our garbage ended up than about my depressing new reality—*we* were considered trash by many of our wealthy, spoiled customers. Retail associates, I soon learned, were an easy target for shoppers' aggression, shoppers who were smugly certain we could never retaliate.

The holidays brought out the bitch in everyone, regardless of gender. On Black Friday, it was as though some internal mechanism had shifted gears, freeing the normally well behaved to act out with impunity. Suddenly—only in those four weeks between Thanksgiving and Christmas—it was all id, all the time! People living in multimillion-dollar mansions, CEOs of some of the nation's largest financial, legal, and corporate offices, people raised in wealth at prep schools and the Ivies where they might have picked up a few manners along the way, now behaved like five-year-olds on a sugar high: tossing new clothing into corners or onto the floor or jamming it into racks, leaving their half-filled, loose-lidded soda and coffee containers teetering on the corners of shelves and tables.

Jared, normally one of our cheeriest staffers, and a retail veteran, stared in disbelief as we tried hopelessly to keep the store tidy and organized. "It's like trying to rake leaves in a windstorm," he said, sighing. We folded and refolded, stacked and restacked the same piles of sweaters, T-shirts, sweats, and pants dozens of times an hour. Thick, bulky ski gloves kept falling off their long, narrow hooks. Slippery wool and fleece scarves slithered onto the floor. My thumbs, dried out from handling fabric all day long, became so dehydrated the skin cracked. They would have bled if I hadn't kept them covered with bandages, unattractive but necessary. Bloodstains on the merch? Not an option.

Every rule of civilized behavior was being broken before our weary eyes. I'd never seen anything like it.

Our greatest pleasure, and our only chance for revenge, became that of negation. We may have crap jobs for low pay, but we had the heady and delicious power of saying, "No."

As in (add fake smile here):

"No, we're out of that color/size/style."

"No, we won't be getting any more."

"No, it doesn't come in black/purple/with pockets."

Saying no felt so damn good! Judging by their stunned expressions, these were people *no* one ever said no to.

Tameisha passed me one afternoon in the corridor to the stockroom, heading back to break the news to one more customer that the black nylon jacket with the hood just wasn't available.

"Gotta go crush their dreams," she said.

"Crush their windpipe is more like it," I replied.

The worst moment that first holiday season was a combination of my inexperience and a nasty customer. I had been helping a woman and her teenage son, who was clearly mentally disabled and grouchy, neither easy to please nor to fit. She was weary, and I patiently helped them both. We headed to the cash wrap, where a long line of customers already stood waiting. I went to ring up my customer and complete the sale, and stood her in front of a scrawny blonde at the front of one long line. It didn't seem right to suddenly push my customer to the back, so to complete the sale graciously and smoothly I stood her at the front of that line.

The result was as shocking and loud as if I'd punched the blonde in the face.

"*What do you think you're doing?*" she shrieked, as much at me as at my shocked customer and her son. "I'm in line here! Who do you think you are, cutting in like that?"

My poor client shriveled, confused and scared. Everyone in line behind the screamer looked miserable, and I knew they were all watching me to see how I would handle it. Would I snap back? Walk away? Burst into tears? Go get a manager?

None of the above.

It was actually my fault, but I wasn't about to admit it—or my new-ness to retail. I asked my customer and her son to stand out of the way, on one side of the cash wrap behind me, as the harpy shouted and cursed me and threatened to call corporate. I got my customer out, trying simultaneously to make Ms. Nuts lower her voice, ring up the sale accurately, and apologize profusely to my poor shopper and her son.

The blonde just wouldn't shut up. It was as though someone had pressed a screaming-bitch button. I rang her up, shaking, desperately wanting to shriek back at her. I was frustrated with myself, and my managers, for allowing this situation to escalate and make my customer—and me—the brunt of such undeserved rage.

Plus the humiliation of being treated like crap in front of a dozen strangers.

The next customer, a young woman, stepped forward, whispering sympathetically, "What a witch!"

Men were always nicer. Maybe because they enjoyed more money, power, status, or time. Maybe it was just some sort of girl thing, all those skinny blondes with ropy arms and size 2 hips and $18,000 wafer-thin gold Cartier watches. These women were the ones who felt compelled to remind us all that they had whatever it took to snag a wealthy man/job/life, while we—poor, pitiable fools in ugly shoes, nylon uniforms, a dead-end job, and plastic-tagged lanyards—clearly did not.

Maybe these women were nastier to us because they were so accustomed to bossing around an entire army of docile, grateful, low-status women—their cooks/nannies/trainers/au pairs/manicurists/babysitters—that they simply mistook us for yet more of their attentive flock.

No matter how rude the men, and a few were pretty horrid, the women were *always* worse.

A middle-aged woman from one of our region's richest towns dumped her $5,000 handbag on the counter, heading off to the dressing room, as she barked, "Look after this." I grew up around old money and I knew the sharpest rebuke in that world is silence. I simply raised my eyebrow in disbelief. She was clearly furious at my perceived insubordination and sullenly carried her bag with her.

I had also started to pick up some of my coworkers' sharper street smarts. I knew perfectly well that if this woman later discovered so much as a used Kleenex had slipped out of her bag, my head, and the company's, would be on the block.

Another woman shopping alone, also about my age, decided to try on a jacket over her sweater on the sales floor. I stood nearby, as always, ready to find her another size or color if needed. As she started to peel off the outer layer again, fearing she might expose some skin, she turned to me and ordered, "Hold my sweater!" As in, hold down the hem of my sweater while I take off this jacket.

Did I *want* to touch her? Did she not know what a weird request this was? Of course, I did it—how could I have refused?

"Please," I said, clearly and loudly, as I held down the hem of her garment with both hands. "Hold my sweater, *please!*" I spoke in the weary, firm tone you'd use with a four-year-old. I didn't care if she tattled to a manager or complained to corporate. She was over the line, and we both knew it. After she left, I told Angie what I'd said. "You *said* that?" she gasped, aghast at my insolence. "What did she say?"

Nothing. She'd said nothing, just as I'd known she would. You could smell the ones who would really escalate a fight. I'd quickly learned how to pick 'em. She was just a garden-variety jerk.

All of us at The North Face, whatever our age, race, or gender, were routinely treated this way. Customers thought nothing of snapping at us with a careless familiarity, as though we were their servants, or possibly disliked, dim-witted relatives.

As a result, the kind shoppers, the fun ones, those who clearly appreciated us, were sometimes deeply moving.

Suzanne, a tall, lean, gorgeous blonde, came into the store in the fall of 2007, just after we'd opened. She was wearing the sort of clothes you only see in Soho or the Marais—a long cardigan and short wool skirt, soft leather boots, all in moody, muted tones of gray and brown, sort of an extremely chic-but-casual fog. We started talking and didn't stop for an hour, while her teenage daughter waited patiently (unheard-of in spoiled local teens), without whining or interrupting. We had so much in common that it was eerie: we were the same age, both of us had lived in the same European city, we were formerly married to high-earning husbands, and perhaps what made us talk for so long and with such quick intimacy was that we both felt out of place in this conservative, manicured, mostly married county. She bought $800 worth of clothes, we traded phone numbers, and she left. I never heard from her, and assumed she'd enjoyed the chat but decided to leave it at that.

As a shopper myself, I'd similarly enjoyed such intimate, long conversations with shopkeepers or associates. It was fun and comforting in that moment, but you didn't always, later, want to become friends or even meet up again. I figured that was what Suzanne had decided, and I didn't want to make her uncomfortable by pushing it.

In this new role, it wasn't as though we were social equals. We'd never discussed this in training, where or how or when you could fraternize with customers outside the store. Maybe management assumed it was none of their business. Or that no customer *would* find us socially or romantically appealing. For once, oddly, there were no rules.

Suzanne was clearly in transition: newly returned to her home country after decades away; becoming a divorcée and single mother; struggling to redefine herself without a husband. I'd been through some of that after my husband, a physician, had walked out of our apartment and our two-year marriage in June 1994, after seven years together. I'd left my native Canada to follow his work, leaving behind dear old friends, a thriving career, my family, and all that I knew. I viscerally understood what a dizzying and disorienting time Suzanne now faced, what writer Abigail Trafford—someone whose book I recommended to her—called, so wisely, "crazy time."

A year later, Suzanne returned, this time with her oldest daughter, a college student. I went over to say hello.

"You're the one!" her daughter exclaimed, clearly excited to meet me. "My mom hasn't stopped talking about you." I was surprised. Could a lowly clerk really have had an impact on this wealthy, worldly woman?

The final moments of our conversation a year earlier had included an unusual request—did I know a good local therapist? I was flattered she thought enough of me to ask my advice. I *did* know such a person, a man I'd seen for years until I couldn't afford his $175/hour, no-insurance fees. He was someone I thought could make a great fit for her: funny, tough, no bullshit. Now she told me gratefully she'd been seeing him for the past year. It was obvious in her confidence and renewed spirit, and I was delighted we'd both been able to help her.

I lived for these moments. Retail, at its rare best, allows total strangers to quickly connect and converse meaningfully. It's really, often, about trust, the merchandise and the sales floor merely the means through which two people, however briefly, can slow down long enough to discover and enjoy common ground. It wasn't an accident that after a twenty-minute conversation with me someone would easily spend $400, or much more. That person had received my careful, individual, and undivided attention, a rarity in any store.

A rarity anywhere, really.

FIVE

THE GOOD NEWS

We'd survived our first holiday season.

It felt good, and showed us that Joe had hired well. We'd gotten along, able to rely on one another in the most frenzied moments when there was zero room for error, when customers lined up eight or ten deep in three weary, foot-tapping lines. Perhaps because it was all new to me, I'd mostly enjoyed the holidays' insanity. Nothing was duller than an empty store. Busy times forced us into, and kept us in, a cooperative team, transforming us from a group of autonomous salespeople into a weaving, bobbing cash-wrap ballet. There might as be many as five or six of us behind the counter at once, working three cash registers but with only two devices to remove sensor tags—detachers—one at each end.

The middle detacher was missing because . . . I'd broken it. Not only had I broken it, I'd done so *on the second-busiest retail night of the year*—Christmas Eve. Thank God, Angie, our soft-spoken assistant manager, the one whose mom was my age, hadn't shouted at me. By now she knew me well enough to know I was a hard worker, not malicious or careless. No one had freaked out or yelled, which I'd expected and knew could certainly have been justified. Having worked for a number of workplace screamers in journalism, I was gratefully surprised.

With only two detachers, we were forced into nonstop cooperation and close physical proximity—whether we wanted it or not. It made for a lot of "Excuse me!" and "Sorry!" as we bumped hips or butts with one another while reaching for bags, boxes, tissue paper, and stickers from more than six cabinets and four drawers. Only some mutual affection and humor, which luckily most of us had, made it bearable.

Thanks to those twenty-four hours of initial training, we now knew our stuff. Initially, I heard from a beleaguered Joe, there had been plenty of infighting and gossip, maybe normal in a group in which so many were young women in their early twenties. There were accusations of sales stolen, things removed from lockers. I avoided gossip. I needed my time in the store to be a refuge from the frustration of my freelance work—the *last* thing I wanted to deal with there was any more drama.

My stepmother had died, at the age of sixty-three, on October 19, at home in her bed, only three weeks after I was hired to work at The North Face. Joe had been gracious, letting me travel back to Toronto even as my coworkers did all the hard physical labor of stocking the store for the opening. It had been a grueling, frightening, angry few months within our family as she'd stared death in the face. My father and her then-twenty-seven-year-old son, her only child, still living at home and in college, desperately did whatever they could to offer solace to her, and to one another. She died the afternoon of my fiancé's fiftieth birthday as I shopped for a dinner party for him planned for that night at a friend's home. We had driven to Toronto from New York to be with my dad and, we hoped, to say our final good-byes to Sandy, whatever her condition. She and I had known one another since I was twelve and I had moved in with her and my father when I was fifteen, for four years. We had never gotten along easily. No matter how hard we tried, we remained very different people and our relationship had never been especially affectionate.

As the end neared, I'd written her a letter, thanking her for her kindnesses to me over the years. It moved her to tears, she told me. But, to my dismay, our final conversation was an argument, and in her last few days she banned us from the house. There would be no deathbed reconciliation.

Now I badly craved some calm and stability. I needed a break from the nightmare of the past eighteen months since her terrible, inevitable diagnosis of late-stage lung cancer.

Working retail in January is a great way to find peace and quiet. It's dead. Shoppers are broke and worn out, staying home in wintry weather—at least in New York—to give their credit cards a well-deserved break. We had little new or fresh to show them, just the same products we'd had in stock since fall, so most of our shoppers then were heading out on ski trips or vacation, were tourists or traveling businessmen, or parents eager to find clothing and accessories to keep their kids warm and dry.

One consistently profitable source of our business was kids' clothing. It was the part I liked least.

The company manufactures many technical products, from mountain-climbing gear to super-light nylon shoes specially designed for kayaking and canoeing. I found these cool, fun, and interesting, but, as someone with no personal exposure to kids, I was bored and out of my depth in the children's department. And only about 10 percent of our store was devoted to kids' clothing, which meant many parents sourly deemed our selection inadequate. Once more, associates took the brunt for decisions made far above our pay grade and many months earlier.

I disliked most of the designs. Girls' jackets, inevitably, came in sickly Easter egg pastels: baby-blue, candy-floss pink, pastel polka dots, white or pale yellow. Some, which were always popular, were a soft, furry-looking fleece that felt like the surface of a stuffed animal. Boys' jackets and accessories were sensible navy, gray, or black, sometimes red. The styling of these garments showed the least imagination of anything we sold, but parents didn't seem to care—if it fit and they could afford it, they were done.

The kids themselves were too often bored, distracted, and danger-ously unsupervised. Pretty much everything in the store could hurt a careless or distracted child (or adult), with sharp metal or wood edges and long, straight, stiff protruding hooks that could do anyone serious damage if they fell or (as one woman did) walked into one. For all our cleaning, the floors were hardly pristine, so kids ducking deep beneath the lowest racks to hide, as they often did, might well find there huge clumps of dirt. And mousetraps. I kept my eyes peeled for them, but occasionally a sensor tag pin lay unnoticed on the floor, another nasty hazard.

None of which, of course, we could effectively point out to parents.

Kids dropped their food and gum and pretzels and drinks every-where, as though the shop were a garbage can, not a shared public space. They ran, shrieked, slid, and dashed around the L-shaped store as if it were a playground. I didn't dare chastise them in front of their parents. If I caught one alone misbehaving, I'd give him or her the stink-eye, hissing, "*I saw that!*"

They didn't care. Most of them had been taught we weren't worth listening to.

The best-behaved, consistently, were European children, whether those living here or visiting on vacation; Greenwich and other wealthy enclaves are filled with investment bankers and the portable families they install for a few years on their London–Hong Kong–Paris circuit. Even two-year-olds were told firmly, calmly, quietly, and clearly when they were misbehaving and what the consequences would be. One couple vis-iting from Iceland came into the store with their two sons, ages eight and twelve. While their parents shopped and I had a long conversation with each of them, the boys waited calmly and politely. No tantrums, no whining, no staring into a cell phone, video game, or PDA, no tapping out texts.

I did enjoy helping older kids. One, a Boy Scout who came in with his dad, grilled me politely about the right size and shape for a backpack he needed for a camping trip. He was touchingly formal and polite, intent on his mission, clearly really excited about his next outdoor adventure. We traded notes about the joys of sleep-away camp—where I had spent my summers age eight to sixteen—and all the cool skills they taught us. I mentioned that, as a journalist, I often write for *Boys' Life*, the Boy Scout magazine, and his eyes lit up. "Do you have a son who's a Boy Scout?" he asked.

His innocent, friendly question hit home. It was sometimes painful to meet a lovely kid and wonder what I'd missed by never having one of my own.

It was fascinating watching children react as their parents spent hundreds of dollars on them. For many, it was something they merely tolerated, clearly bored. Sometimes, not often, they were deeply appreciative. One day a woman walked into the store trailed by three very pretty young girls, maybe ten, twelve, and fifteen, clearly her daughters. I recognized her immediately as a famous model now married to an equally famous singer; in our suburban store, we very rarely saw celebrities. They had to be enormously wealthy, and I wondered how she and her girls would behave. She wore a hefty emerald-cut diamond, a warning light, as many of those who did were the rudest and most demanding.

She bought a jacket for herself and another for one of the daughters. "Thank you, Mommy," her daughter said, rising on tiptoes to kiss her. I was stunned, so unusual were her gratitude and good manners.

* * *

I was settling into this new life, grateful to have found a refuge that was calm, quiet, consistent, reliable, and predictable. No matter how small my paycheck, it arrived in my bank account by direct deposit every other Friday. As the recession deepened and writing work became more elusive, and as many clients cut their budgets and fees, I increasingly counted on that money.

My weeks, now, once more had a rhythm. I was anchored, earning a paycheck from a well-known, well-liked brand. I once more had a professional identity and a new set of skills accumulating with every shift. Every Tuesday, now, I had a place to go and people relying on me to show up, to be on time, and to do my job well. I had coworkers I liked and a boss who was funny, warm, and down-to-earth. I had a free, comfortable, company-supplied uniform.

It seemed like a lot to me.

Since I'd begun working there, I heard a refrain from friends, family, colleagues, neighbors—anyone, really, who knew me well: "Are you *still* there?"

No one could quite imagine me, short-tempered, impatient, easily bored, actually enjoying a low-level, low-wage service job. I was surprised, too. I didn't expect to like it, certainly not to like it a lot. But I did. I had never realized how hungry I was for regular human contact that wasn't fraught with drama (my family), or ridiculous competition (journalism) or perpetual fear and insecurity (freelancing).

I loved the constant variety of our customers, and their wildly differing needs, whether a jacket stretchy enough to cover a government agent's Glock nine-millimeter pistol or warm, knee-high black wool socks for the private jet pilots who told me they got cold standing around the tarmac waiting for their bosses. I liked meeting students of all ages, from middle school to graduate school, needing new backpacks. As someone who had traveled the world, I relished trading stories about my own adventures backpacking through Europe, hiking the Andes, and snorkeling in Fiji— all of which our customers were eager to do and happy to hear about.

I'd played many sports and had lived in a brutally cold place—Montreal in the winter—so also knew and could confidently recommend which products worked best for skiing, skating, snowboarding, or just walking the dog in February.

I loved being the authority, knowing what we had to offer and, as instructed explicitly in training, referring customers to other retailers for products we didn't make or might not have in stock. I also appreciated how hard it was for women, especially curvy ones my size, to find attractive, comfortable, well-designed athletic clothing, so I often referred them to Athleta or Title Nine, two companies—one of them woman-owned—that are my personal favorites. The North Face was wise to encourage this freedom, as shoppers sought our help, not a vague, uninterested shrug.

I really liked knowing, for once and without any doubts, that I *had* been helpful. Journalism isn't a field filled with warm, nurturing people sharing hugs. Praise is very rare, criticism the norm. Some of the people you interview are super-controlling, others scared to death or simply hate journalists. Others call up—as one government PR flack did—and scream at the top of their lungs, just for the fun of trying to intimidate a female reporter into docility.

However weird it sounds, it was often much more fun selling T-shirts than writing for national publications.

Only one friend, a woman twenty-three years younger, working in a Canadian bank as a part-time manager while completing her PhD, really understood. Our service jobs offered us both a needed respite from our difficult families and demanding primary work. She, too, craved a place where most people behaved politely and predictably, where customers, coworkers, and managers were actually appreciative of our hard work and good skills. Unlike some of our own relatives, total strangers—there—valued us. Some even wrote attaboy letters or praised us to our faces, in front of our coworkers and our managers.

Our lower-wage, lower-status jobs, then, no matter how mundane or unglamorous on paper, filled other real needs. Not just income or transferable skills, but a reliable emotional satisfaction that our families and our primary, slower, and more cerebral work—hers in academia, mine in journalism—didn't offer.

"*I make people happy!*" she'd exult, when we compared our part-time service jobs. She loved being able to help someone get a loan or obtain a mortgage, walking a confused customer through an intimidating or complicated process. "They walk in with a problem, they tell me about it, and I solve it," she said. "That feels great."

She was right. I so appreciated this job's simplicity—show up, work hard, go home, get paid.

I also liked having a uniform. It changed seasonally. In winter it was either a nylon long-sleeved shirt or sweater. In summer, it was whatever short-sleeved shirt we could squeeze into; for those of us with a sizable chest, this was difficult or impossible, as so much North Face clothing was cut so small. Even the women's XL was button-straining. (Men's sizes, of course, went up to XXL.) Between the hot lights and running around carrying armloads of stuff, I sweated a lot. I couldn't imagine having to wear stockings or a skirt or heels, staining and ruining my own clothes. We wore light, supportive, and comfortable sneakers or boots, two free pairs twice a year.

Knowing I'd be a brand ambassador for the next seven hours also gave me a regular reason to dress up a bit, put on some makeup and earrings and perfume. I know what *I* expect when I shop, and if I was going to sell $500 jackets or $200 boots to affluent shoppers I needed to be well groomed and attractive. No matter how the rest of my life was going, I had to be "on" and ready to work. Being needed, being relied upon, even for simple tasks at a low wage, was balm to my soul.

It's too easy, when you work alone at home for years, to get lazy, wearing only loose, comfy clothing like sweats and slippers. In really bad weather, sometimes for several days in a row I wouldn't even leave our building, sometimes exiting the apartment only to get the mail.

Only one of our uniforms was uncomfortable and unflattering, a sky-blue fleece hoodie so thick and hot it felt and looked like a baby blanket. Alone among my younger coworkers, I faced a unique challenge—occasional hot flashes. I wore the hoodie only once, the night a severe hot flash left me soaked with sweat. I went to the bathroom, dried myself with paper towels, and bought a cotton men's T-shirt off the floor for something fresh to change into. My short hair was dripping with perspiration; Angie, kindly, wondered if I'd stuck my head beneath the tap midshift.

Now getting ready to go to the store every week gave me a focus, a destination, and a friendly group of colleagues. I liked hearing how Tam's young son was doing, how Carl, studying at a local community college, was enjoying his psychology classes, what weekend plans Joe had. Partly because Joe, too, had been married and divorced, and because he was only seven years my junior, and because of his athletic prowess and passion for travel, he and I had by far the most in common. We'd each grown up in well-off, socially connected families, had each attended college, had each traveled widely. I had lived in France for a year, and had thrived there on a fellowship; he had lived in—and loved—Germany while serving in the military. Like me, he longed to go back to Europe to live. Very few of our associates had left the United States, and if they had, it was usually to visit relatives in Puerto Rico or Mexico or the Dominican Republic.

Joe and I often joked about our clunky old cathode-ray tube television sets. Everyone we knew had, or desperately wanted, a huge, sleek flat-screen. Not us, we told ourselves, laughing. That $800 or $1,200 or $1,500 to us represented the chance to flee, the price of an airfare to somewhere cool and far away. Those were our shared values. In the stuffy, materialistic, image-obsessed county where we both lived and worked, one I'd chosen for its proximity to Manhattan but not for its inherent suburban charms, we were considered weird for our obsession with more adventure and further exploration, our mutual love of getting as far away from the Gucci-Lexus-Hamptons crowd for as long as possible and as often as we could afford it.

In Joe, I'd finally found a kindred spirit. I felt lucky to have found someone who so often saw the world, and valued it, as I did.

Now, knowing I had to clock in by one o'clock sharp—we'd get in trouble if we were even five minutes late—galvanized me to organize my day and my week. I started out working Tuesday nights and Wednesday during the days, but soon dropped that second shift, as I could easily earn that same $75 if I hustled harder for more writing assignments. (Retail will, sooner or later, do that to you, spur you to extra effort to minimize your time there.) And my feet ached so badly at the end of each shift that I couldn't go back barely twelve hours later and start it all again.

As my in-store sales skills developed, I lost some of my fear of calling or e-mailing new clients for potential writing and editing work. Thanks to my growing comfort approaching total strangers, quickly gaining their trust or confidence as I did each week on the sales floor, sales of my own work were picking up.

By midwinter of 2008, I'd already seen I could sell, and do it well. Coming home after a long night pushing costly ski jackets, pants, or sweaters to a parade of strangers, some initially challenging or dubious, showed me I *did* know how to sell. I just had to get over my fear of rejection and get on with it. Selling mass-produced merchandise finally made it clear to me—*it's all just product*, whether my own story idea or a pair of gloves. I had wasted too much energy for too many years personalizing rejection. I *could* sell. I just had to bring the same level of enthusiasm and cheery confidence to my own ideas and skills as I did to the store's nylon and fleece.

Knowing exactly what I'd accomplished every night—my UPTs (units per transaction, the higher the better), my sales per hour, my daily total—showed me, my bosses, and my coworkers what I was made of. I liked that clarity, a lot.

I'd entered a new world. For the first time in my life, having always worked only in journalism, whose value judgments are hopelessly subjective, I and my managers and their bosses and all my colleagues could and did track and measure one another's progress. Everyone's sales figures, and every metric associated with them—sales per hour, average value of each sale, how many of our sales were later returned, UPTs— were posted each week on a wall near the stockroom. We knew who was working hard and who, even with plenty of hours, still wasn't pulling their weight. The software systems that tracked our every move also gave me reassuringly clear and verifiable data, undeniable proof of what I had accomplished.

I'd never worked in a place that made individual effort, and results, so brutally public. But, being so competitive, I liked it. I was doing fine and everyone could see it.

It felt odd heading to the mall every week, because for years I had avoided it as a shopper. But I was finally getting to know it, and discovered a few simple pleasures within it. After years disoriented by its huge multilevel parking lot, I now knew exactly where to park to step out of the elevator, turn a sharp left, and sprint for the store with seconds left to clock in on time. Or I'd head to Starbucks and pick up a medium Earl Grey tea, with two tea bags and lots of skim milk, to stash inside my locker. I'd learned quickly how thirsty we got and how comforting it was to sip something soothing, hot, and familiar throughout my shift. I usually brought unsalted almonds to gnaw on for a healthy, low-calorie, and quickly gulped source of energy. Fresh fruit was too difficult to eat fast, and too messy—my hands and fingers needed to stay clean for handling the merch or taking customers' money or credit cards.

On my unpaid hour-long break I'd slip back through the looking glass (my name badge stowed in my pocket) and morph back into being a shopper. I'd step into Anthropologie, still one of my favorite stores, whose associates don't wear badges. Their space in this mall had enormous windows facing the street, so on even the cloudiest day plenty of natural light poured in. Their music was quirky, interesting, and low-key. Their floors were wide, soft planks of wood, their wildly creative walls and displays ever-changing as the store staff remade them to their own designs. I loved the store's trademark mix of fragrant European soaps, long cardigans, gleaming glassware and dishes, beaded Indian headbands, pottery doorknobs, and photo, poetry, and design books. The place, however cannily curated, oozed creativity and (in its own deliberate mass-market kind of way) a highly profitable celebration of individuality.

There, even in fifteen minutes, I could lose myself in a dreamy reverie.

Because I knew the store so well, I could find what I wanted quickly. I also noticed—as an annoyed shopper—they never seemed to have enough associates at the cash wrap. I now saw every store as not just a place to buy stuff, but a workplace. I began to watch associates and managers with a different eye. Did they look harried? Happy? Were they attentive and helpful?

I'd become a dual personality, both a hardworking associate and a demanding consumer. Because I now knew what it takes to staff a store properly, to train well, and how to give attentive service, I knew—*it's not that difficult!* If I and my coworkers could do it, why couldn't everyone else? Sufficient staff, anywhere, was rare, good service even more so, and I began to resent it now that I was working so hard for my wages. When I shopped, I wanted to enjoy it! And a lacy little $70 T-shirt was now the trade-off for an entire shift's labor.

I've always been frugal, but now, for the first time since college, when I lived alone on a very tight budget, I truly understood the value of a dollar and what slogging labor it can take to earn it. It cost me $9 to park at the mall (up from $8 when I first started working there). If I bought a meal at the food court, it was $8 to $12. Two hours of my labor—gone. It was a sobering reminder that this part-time job was still, fortunately, one way for me to make a living. Not the *only* way. I still had other skills that could command higher wages and hoped, soon enough, to be using them again.

I'd stop into the mall's beauty supply shop to pick up a new nail polish or high-end hair conditioner or comb, each an affordable but useful little treat. Being able to spend even a little bit, to be served instead of serving, buoyed my mood and reminded me that I, too, was a consumer. I, too, could soak up someone else's attention before going back into our store and giving it myself.

Like all people who work on their feet in retail, I really needed that break. Being "on" for four or five or six hours in a row was tiring. I needed a chance to let my face relax, to not have to smile or say, "Hey!" within ten seconds of spotting a new customer. To remember I was still *me*, not just employee 431877.

I was enjoying getting to know my coworkers, too.

Despite our many significant differences—in age, race, education, background, and neighborhood—we mostly got along well. I credit our manager, Joe, for this, having weeded out in his hiring and our training anyone who was too rough-edged, raucous, or unwilling to learn. Almost everyone, whether in their twenties, thirties, or forties, brought a calm geniality to their work—or, for some, a resignation that this was their lot for now and they might as well do it right. Some were people I'd never have spoken to socially (and two just plain nasty), but we knew our jobs and we knew what behavior was expected. I couldn't imagine by what specific criteria Joe had chosen us all, but I was always struck by how relatively harmoniously we got along.

It was a far cry from the prickly, self-protective vibe of almost every newsroom or magazine office I'd ever worked in. There, it was all-ego-all-the-time, the politicking relentless. In my last job at the *Daily News*, I'd tried many times, fruitlessly, to strike up a friendly conversation with colleagues. One woman, whom senior managers considered a star, refused to speak to me when I wandered over to her desk one quiet afternoon to chat.

Only the very few who were solidly ensconced, or the safely off-the-radar administrative/support staff there, were friendly, and I was grateful to them for it. One man, the janitor who came around to empty our garbage cans, was a strikingly handsome Hispanic man somewhere in his thirties. None of my colleagues, that I saw, ever said thank you or even acknowledged his daily presence. I always made a point of saying hello.

In this new job, then, no matter what it paid, I was eager to fit in and get along, to make sure I wasn't—as I so clearly had been at the newspaper—a pariah.

My coworkers here seemed to like me. They saw that I worked hard. I swept the floors and folded shirts and made my sales goals. I pulled my weight. I liked most of them and looked forward to my time with them. Which, it turned out, is *crucial* when your job is low-level, offers you no chance to develop managerial skills or take on new responsibilities, or when the shift's toughest challenge is to sensor-tag twenty ski jackets or rehang forty sweaters.

Unlike journalism, which, we often joked, paid many of us best in "psychic income" (that is, prestige or national visibility or the attention of those a few rungs above us socially or professionally), retail work offered few pleasures beyond a small paycheck. Only the companionship and camaraderie of your coworkers, I soon grew to appreciate, gets you through. I really liked working with Jared, a goofy, easygoing twenty-four-year-old. He was always funny, almost never in a foul mood. He lived with his girlfriend, a fashion designer, and they both had specific and ambitious plans far beyond the confines of the store, the company, and the mall.

I worked almost every Tuesday night with Tameisha, gazelle-slim and graceful, a dark-skinned black woman with almond-shaped eyes who was one of only three full-time employees, and the only full-time female associate. She was living, she told me, with her mother and three-year-old son in the same public housing project where she had grown up. Only thanks to her mother's free child care could she even afford to work.

She had a dignity and formality to her manner that I valued, as it reminded me of Canada, where I grew up, a place where people typically are more reserved and less eager to open up quickly or expect that from others. She always said "Good morning" and "Thank you."

When the store opened, she wore a minuscule diamond, a chip, really, on her left hand, clearly an engagement ring. It soon disappeared. Tam was a deeply private woman, not one to spill her innermost thoughts or feelings. After many months working with her, I mustered the nerve to ask what had happened to the ring.

"Are you still engaged?"

"No," she said disgustedly. "I just can't rely on him. He won't pay child support. He can't keep a job. He moved to Buffalo and wanted me to move with him. What am I going to do there? Far away from my mother? Why would I follow him when he doesn't even handle his responsibilities?"

Tam had worked three jobs while pregnant, even then running up credit card debt as she tried to support herself and her baby on minimum-wage work. Now, saddled with a mid-four-figures debt, she was living with her mother, eager to move out on her own.

"This isn't the life I planned," she said. "Living with my mother at twenty-eight!"

Clearly frustrated by her life, she was equally determined to make the best of it. She was generous with her coworkers, buying gifts for them and their children. She was meticulous about the store and its displays. She fussed endlessly over her son, buying him clothes and toys and an elaborate birthday cake. I loved her disdain for the corporate BS we were often handed in training and store meetings. She could be wickedly funny, muttering imprecations sotto voce that cracked me up every time.

"Low wages 'R' us!" she hissed one afternoon.

But she was also moody and mercurial. I never knew which Tam would await me when I arrived at the store. Sometimes she was great company, wryly funny, teasing, and playful, sometimes withdrawn, monosyllabic, and barely civil. She had attended a local college and had a four-year degree. She talked of going into medicine, perhaps into nursing, but commuting ninety minutes each way to our store and this job allowed her little time, cash, or energy to pursue an advanced degree or better skills that might free her from dull, low-wage work. She was clearly bright, bored with the brain-numbing, unvarying routines that define selling mass-marketed clothing year after year: open enormous cardboard boxes, unsheathe product from slick plastic wrapping, attach sensor tags, fold or hang them in the areas chosen months earlier by faraway bosses with militarily precise ideas how the store must look.

There was, at our company anyway, simply no room for individual ideas or creativity.

* * *

There are, of course, longtime retail employees perfectly happy in the industry. If you can find the right fit, it's a great place for people who—as the song says—love people.

Angel Silva, a Costco employee in San Diego working there for the second time, was thrilled to rejoin a well-known, well-respected company that treats him well and pays him $50,000 a year. He's not leaving again anytime soon. For many people, a retail job, as it did for me, can offer a wanted refuge, certainly when it pays a decent wage or offers its part-timers health benefits, which a few retailers do, such as Costco, Starbucks, Trader Joe's, The Container Store, and the grocery store chain Wegmans.

Silva, a thirty-five-year-old married father of two in San Diego, worked at Costco for three years, from 2002 to 2005, as a forklift operator, making $50,000. He enjoyed the job, but wanted to boost his earnings, obtained his Realtor's license, and began selling real estate. He earned $90,000 in 2005 and 2006. "But in 2007, the market started to decline and I was barely making it, with about fifty thousand dollars. In 2009, I think I made about thirty-five thousand. I was doing mostly short sales or selling to people who just weren't qualifying for mortgages anymore." With a family to support, Silva needed help fast, and got it—by reapplying to his old company, which was happy to rehire him in July 2009, this time as a quality control supervisor. He soon won a promotion and is once more making a steady, reliable $50,000 a year. He's relieved to have found a decent job with a thriving company, a needed respite from the daily stress of selling real estate in a terrible economy.

"I'm not growing as much as I'd like to be, but at least I'm not going down, for now. I don't plan on quitting my Costco job anymore for now. I'm so grateful to the managers there who gave me back my job," says Silva. "It's hard to get a job out there! Any kind of job. It's hard!"

Silva discovered that selling real estate—with his first commission check of $8,000 a heady victory—was a lot tougher than he'd hoped. "It was a completely different type of work. The hardest part for me was how to talk to people. I wasn't too talkative. I am now!

"Selling real estate really looks easier than it is. You work very, very hard and every transaction is different. In real estate, you have to supervise every transaction, with fifteen to twenty people involved. At the end, clients always complain about something."

Now he supervises only seven employees and the work, and pace, is steady and predictable. No more working nights or weekends. Surrounded once more by friendly coworkers, not other Realtors in the same office competing hard for the same shrinking pool of clients, Silva says he's "relaxing. I want some time out! As soon as I clock out of work here, I'm out, just like everyone else."

Would he quit retail for a second time? "This time I'm going to be more careful. I don't think so."

For Jacqueline Alvarino, who works in a Limited store selling women's clothing, retail fits her needs just fine. A 2009 graduate of California State, Fullerton, in modern Latin American history, she hopes to obtain her PhD and teach or work for a nonprofit organization. She was offered a full ride at Vanderbilt University, but decided to take a break from academia and began working as an associate in June 2009.

"Sometimes I look at what my friends are doing—one is on a Fulbright in Chiapas, one is in law school—and feel a sense of envy, but then I think I wouldn't be doing as well as I could. I'd be lackluster and half-assing the job and half-assing my classes. Right now the desire and energy for more education just isn't there."

She makes $11.50 an hour, a sum that impressed her, as many local retailers are paying only $8 to $9 per hour. She now knows, no matter how "unskilled" associate work is said to be, that it's not. "You have to be charismatic and smooth. You have to *sell*."

She enjoys her coworkers, who are all female, and her managers. "They're very understanding and really, really help us. I love it here! I always feel appreciated." Her coworkers, whom she calls "darlings," range from high school age to thirty-seven. And, like my bank manager friend and me, Alvarino relishes doing a different sort of labor, work that *isn't* complex or intellectually demanding. "It's not rocket science."

At Richards, an upscale men's and women's clothing store in Greenwich, Connecticut, working retail is another world entirely. While this bare-knuckled industry too often offers customers and associates alike the bumpy ride of a banged-up junker, Richards feels like a gleaming new Bentley (whose company showroom is just around the corner).

Owner Jack Mitchell, trim and lively at seventy-one, still sells on the floor. With a master's degree in Chinese history from Berkeley, he has, as you'd expect, an eye for beauty and detail. Tall flowering branches stood around the main floor in vases, spare and simple, the day we met. The Rolling Stones played on the store's sound system.

That rainy March morning, Mitchell wore tobacco-colored suede driving shoes and thick gray ragg wool socks, gray flannel trousers, a Cartier *ballon* watch, a pale blue striped shirt and a light yellow silk tie I thought was Hermès, with its tiny repeated designs—instead, it's his own "Hug" logo.

To maintain the excellence that is his brand, Mitchell is extremely careful about whom he hires. "It's all about the personal relationships," he told me. He receives "several" great applicants every month, understandably eager to work in an attractive store selling luxury goods like Loro Piana cashmere, Hermès, Zegna, and Escada, as well as jewelry at five-figure prices. Associates here can earn a very serious salary.

Mitchell requires seven to eight interviews before hiring for any one of his stores. "You have to really be able to handle public exposure, to handle whatever comes to you. You have to be a true people person and be able to handle the interactions," he said. That really means interacting with a very narrow subset of clients, the nation's wealthiest and most demanding shoppers: professional athletes, hedge-fund managers, elected officials, network television stars.

"I only want people who want this as a career. That's why we have so many interviews," he said. While Mitchells/Richards/Marshs are not on commission, an associate selling $1 million worth of merchandise a year stands to earn anywhere between $60,000 and $100,000-plus yearly, he said.

The store uses a Customer Accumulation System, which carefully tracks what customers buy, when, and why. The retail truism applies— 80 percent of their business is done with 20 percent of their customers, so "you've got to get to know them." Associates learn the names, ages, and hobbies of not only their clients, but their clients' children, grand-children, and in-laws.

Judy Brooks, fifty-one, has sold at Richards for eleven years after working, much less happily, for a major department store. The mother of a twelve-year-old son, she has dark, cropped hair and a friendly intensity. She studied sociology at Ithaca College and didn't know what she wanted to do, so she chose retail.

She was shocked, and crushed, by her first job—working the Christ-mas rush. "I cried! I couldn't believe how mean people could be. You get tired and people are yelling and screaming at you." Managers were over-worked and demands to sell *moremoremoremore* were relentless. "There, it's all about the numbers. It's how the system works. Here, I know my clients. I'm going to dress them for success, go through their closets. This sort of attention, and service, does not exist anywhere else. I've walked into Barneys [an upscale Manhattan department store] and it doesn't happen."

Brooks appreciates the autonomy Mitchell's system gives her, cer-tainly in contrast to the nonstop pressure she worked under elsewhere. For her, this retail job is a haven: "I feel I can be *me* and not put on a cor-porate façade."

For Waldy Peralta, retail is, literally, a world away from the small rural Dominican Republic town where he was born and lived to the age of nine, before his family moved to the New York City suburbs.

"I came from a place with outhouses and rivers," he says. Peralta, lean, handsome, and soft-spoken, began working part-time when he was seventeen in our local hardware store, Goldberg's. There are few jobs more macho than a hardware store, and few men *less* macho than Peralta.

A hard worker and quick learner, he was offered a full-time job right out of high school—at $42,000, plus a bonus and an additional $2,000 at Christmas. "No one coming out of *college* makes that!" he says proudly. "I loved it. It's a small town and everyone knew my name. People are the reason I do what I do. I love being around them."

Now twenty-eight, he sells perfumes at Bloomingdale's in Manhattan. "I spritz!" he says, laughing easily. "I went from so butch to so gay—I love it!" Peralta *is* gay, and, as a result, his conservative family has cut him off. His young boss at the hardware store, Gregg Goldberg, whose grandfather opened the store in 1904 and who lives in an apartment over the shop, "is like a father figure to me. He taught me to pitch and catch a ball, how to throw a punch."

Now living in Manhattan, Peralta earns $50,000 a year selling brands like Narciso Rodriguez, Issey Miyake, Jean-Paul Gaultier, and John Varvatos. He's employed not by the department store, but by a company called Beauté Prestige International.

Retail, he says, is a perfect fit for him. "I like people. I *love* people. I like to be the nice guy."

He left the hardware store after ten years "because I wanted to grow with a company. I wanted something bigger and better." He was hired in October 2008, in the depths of the recession.

Retail also works so well for Peralta because he's dyslexic, which makes white-collar office work demanding, and reading and writing painfully difficult. "I'm visual and tactile. I learn by listening and looking. In the hardware store, I'd memorize the size and feel and shape of the hardware."

He does admit that retail, standing on his feet and confined to a small physical space, is "physically exhausting." And customers can be horrible. "We treat them with the utmost respect, like royalty, even if they're wrong. I don't mind it. If they're happy, they'll come back."

Long-term, Peralta plans to leave hammers and cologne far behind— and work as a high school guidance counselor. "I take care of people."

Those who most enjoy retail often own the store. So I spoke to two men, owners of their own small businesses—a pharmacy and a gourmet shop, both of which I frequent—to ask them what it's like.

Aqeel Ghouri runs Tarrytown Pharmacy, a small, narrow space on a busy street in my suburban town twenty-five miles north of New York City. He took over in August 2006 after the previous owner was sentenced to two to six years in prison for Medicaid fraud. That made for a tough start—would local shoppers, dismayed that their trust in their jovial druggist had been so betrayed, try the store again? And his shop sits only two doors away from a competing CVS.

An upbeat, high-energy guy, none of this daunted him. Ghouri, who trained in his native Pakistan, had already worked for many years in retail, for a Manhattan grocery store chain and a regional drugstore chain. He ran an electronics store in the mid-1980s, and even sold fur and leather in the Bronx. He became a pharmacist in 1993. A gentle, handsome man whose thick black beard is salted with gray, he's not one to mince words.

"Retail is brutal! It is!" he says, laughing. "Everyone who walks in thinks you're their slave. They think they can dictate anything they want just because you're behind the counter." It's not unique to the United States, he adds—when he worked in Medina, Saudi Arabia, it was "same job, same thing."

Ghouri is the kind of person patient and passionate enough to—as he did with me—sit down and draw a diagram to explain how vitamins are metabolized. He has three daughters, one a pharmacy student.

"I love retail. It's a challenge to handle these people. I can handle the nastiest customer in the world." Like Peralta, Ghouri also cherishes the small-town pleasure of "knowing ninety-nine percent of my customers personally." His compassion is key when dealing with clients who are often scared and/or in pain. "If you're in pain, you're already burned up! You've seen doctors, you have an injury, you've fought traffic. You've already got all that nonsense going on in your life. We have to be willing to take you as is."

Retail associates get nothing near the pay, nor the respect, they deserve, he agrees. "There's tremendous skill involved! You have to be able to convert shoppers into customers. Conversion is not easy."

He's taken a hit financially to build his business, down from the $120,000 a year he earned working for others. But Ghouri clearly loves his work. "People respect me. They respect my behavior, my knowledge, how I deliver my knowledge, and how I customize it to them."

"I love to serve," he says. As someone who's sat in his store weeping in pain while awaiting a prescription for my osteoarthritis, I know he does.

Hassan Jarane, similarly, exudes a gentle, welcoming warmth to his appreciative customers. A former commercial photographer, this father of two young sons owns Mint, a two-hundred-square-foot gourmet food shop with a cheery red-and-white-striped awning, its door covered with clear plastic strips, making it feel like you're entering a Tunisian souk. A bright red wooden bench sits outside, in summer beside it is an enormous old-fashioned, self-serve glass jar of lemonade. His shop is a riot of visual, sensual pleasures: Moroccan ceramic platters on one wall, barrels of spicy olives and candied walnuts, dried apricots and dates, a wicker basket stacked with fresh baguettes, jewel-toned bottles of hot sauce and vinegar. Within seconds he offers everyone a fistful of candied walnuts or a creamy slice of cheese.

Here I've happily dropped $12 for a small bottle of balsamic glaze or lavender honey, the sort of splurge I'd never make in a chain store. I like buying from Jarane, because I really like knowing when I hand over my money exactly where it's going. Every penny I spend there helps to keep an independent store open, our main street vibrant, and a solo businessman thriving.

He opened Mint in 2003 with no previous retail experience. He had worked in an upscale restaurant and grew up watching his mother run a catering business in his native Morocco and Belgium. "After 9/11, I decided it was time for me to change to something different," he says simply. The store has been a success since it opened on Christmas Eve. "There was a line outside," he says, sounding a little surprised. Tarrytown's scenic main street has been used for film shoots, so his customers have included actress Debra Winger, Keanu Reeves, and Robert De Niro.

Like Ghouri, Jarane offers his suburban shoppers much more than merchandise—which they can find elsewhere. What they *can't* find are these men, their skill, experience, and charming personalities a welcome and attentive break from coldly impersonal chain stores too often poorly staffed by the underpaid and indifferent.

"It's human to human," he says simply. "It's fun to share something. You've got to have a passion for it."

To his dismay, Jarane also finds good customer service rare and elusive. "We're not a customer-oriented people. We're lazy and we're treated like shit. When I'm shopping, I expect service! Don't give me an attitude! I'm spending my money here." He closed his second shop because he had such difficulty finding and keeping workers who met his high standards—even offering $12 per hour plus tips. "And they were fed!"

But Jarane loves running a "mom-and-pop" store; like Ghouri, he knows his customers by name. "If you're short one or two dollars, it's okay. At a mall store, you can't be short a penny. It's an industrial, disposable mind-set."

"I loved retail," agrees Reba Holley, who for twenty-three years ran a framing and needlework shop in Hamilton, New Jersey, with her husband Hoyt. Now working full-time as a medical test sales rep, Reba misses running her own store and the emotional connections it forged.

"Customers mostly were framing for something happy, like a baby's birth, wedding pictures, a memory of a fabulous trip, military service medals. I loved my customers. In general, people don't frame unless they can afford it, and it's usually something special. They loved that I always wanted to hear the story behind their art, certificate, or picture. And we made finding the perfect treatment a team effort. I got such a charge out of putting something creative together and hearing, 'That is so much better than I expected' or 'You were right, I'm glad I took your advice' when the picture was picked up. Of course, most people had a budget, but that was part of the challenge—finding a beautiful frame job within the parameters the customer set. I loved the creativity involved."

I had always dreamed of opening my own small store one day, with prices from $5 to $500, making even small splurges possible. I love to entertain, so it would probably be housewares, a mix of things old and new. Now, having seen the other side of the cash wrap, I've lost any illusions about how much I could really learn about this business while working for others, at least while working for a major corporation squeezed by Wall Street, determined to pump out product.

If I am ever to really enjoy the more creative side of working in retail, it seems, I'll have to find the nerve, and the capital, to do it on my own.

SIX

WEATHERING THE RECESSION

We wondered when, exactly, the recession would hit. By the fall of 2008, our store had been open for a year and—despite increasingly gloomy headlines and predictions of economic doom—our sales remained strong. Shoppers arrived in our narrow doorway so laden with shopping bags they looked like boats with pontoons. If there was trouble in our little suburban paradise, it wasn't yet evident in our mall.

But retail, never the most appealing industry in a healthy economy, would soon reap a new and valuable windfall from the economic downturn—other displaced, desperate, and highly educated workers out of work and out of other options.

That fall, unemployment jumped to 10 percent. Workers, once feeling secure with their jobs, skills, or industries, had bought homes with only a 5 or even 0 percent down payment, locked into balloon or variable rate mortgages. Now many found themselves facing higher housing costs just as their unemployment benefits were running out. For millions, then, even the dull, hard, low-wage work of retail—something they, like I, would never previously have even considered midcareer and midlife—started to look like a good option. By that point, after six or twelve or eighteen months pounding the pavement in vain, any job looked appealing.

I saw it happening across our store counter. Typically, our only job applicants were black or Hispanic, usually in their early twenties. Now even middle-class white men, college-age, were respectfully asking for applications, checking back with us for possible openings.

One day a woman my age started chatting as I rang up her purchase. "What's it like working here?" she asked. I knew what she was really asking, since people never cared what it was like unless they were thinking of crossing the cash wrap themselves.

I told her, in general terms, that I enjoyed it and why. But it was clear that she, as I did, had midlife responsibilities, a mortgage or kids heading off to college. "The money is terrible," I warned her, and told her what we made. She grimaced. Who could blame her?

"I just lost my job," she said. She had worked for more than twenty years at a local hotel. She received no severance pay and little warning. The maximum monthly unemployment benefit in New York State, I knew and she was about to discover, is a bad joke, certainly for anyone previously high-earning and for almost anyone living near Manhattan and paying a tremendous premium in rent or real estate costs for the privilege. New York State unemployment benefits totaled $1,600 a month, a sum that would barely cover the rent on a crummy studio in Manhattan or the monthly taxes on a decent suburban house. Even if you were just job-searching, heading into the city to network or for interviews, a monthly commuter train pass from my town into Manhattan cost $236.

Those now out of work, certainly after their benefits expired, had fewer and fewer choices. In 2009, the number of retail applicants over the age of fifty-five jumped by 25 percent, reported Kronos, a workforce management firm; retailers were hiring only three workers for every hundred job applications they received, a 57 percent reduction from 2006. The industry had already cut more than 850,000 jobs since early 2008.

The rate of U6ers, a Labor Department term for those who have stopped looking for work or who can't find full-time jobs, hit a record 17.4 percent in October 2008. (By late May 2010, it would have dropped only 0.5 percent.) The U6 crowd includes everyone officially unemployed plus "marginally attached workers"—including people who are employed part-time because that's all they can get. Many of these workers are part-time only by default. All would prefer, and need, full-time jobs with decent pay and benefits, but there were few to be had.

By January 2009, the recession had hit our store as well—all the part-time workers saw their hours severely cut, mine to only five hours a week. If things were this tight in our store, I doubted they'd be much better anywhere else. Now that the storm had hit, best to batten the hatches and stay put for a while.

Millions of us, many highly educated, with law degrees, PhDs, MBAs, and decades of experience working for major organizations, were now competing for a rapidly shrinking pool of professional-level opportunities, like Joel Lueck and Jim Bartley, IT professionals in Raleigh, North Carolina. Both are devout Christians, both long married, each with two children in their early twenties.

Lueck, fifty-three, had worked for eighteen years for Nortel, earning, with bonuses and other benefits, between $95,000 and $100,000. He was laid off in May 2008, with severance that covered him until December 2008. He began networking through local church and business groups, both to find a new job and to stay busy, but soon needed a regular income and a place to go.

A new friend, Jim Bartley, whom he had met through a job seekers' networking group, had an idea: they'd split the overnight shift at a local grocery store. The pay? Eight dollars an hour.

Bartley, then forty-eight, had recently lost his IT job of almost ten years. Then earning between $120,000 and $140,000 as a global sales manager, he typically traveled to Taiwan, Japan, Italy, and France. "I guess, kind of arrogantly, the day I was laid off I thought I'd have two or three people call me saying they wanted to give me a job offer," he recalls. "I thought I was going to have a nice little vacation and would go back to a job making more money than at my last job."

That first day turned into three months, then into the summer, by which point he'd had twenty-one day-long job interviews, each one fruitlessly raising his hopes.

To stay busy and earn steady cash, Bartley refereed fifteen soccer games a week, each paying $50 a game, a healthy $3,000 a month. "It was really taking a toll on me! I was living on ibuprofen because my body hurt all the time.

"October 2008 was the 9/11 of the recession," Bartley recalls. His weekly meeting of fellow job seekers had ballooned from forty people to more than five hundred. It was time for drastic action.

Lueck and Bartley, two midlife, former six-figure-earning managers, now wooed a dubious grocery store manager into offering them $8 an hour to split the perennially unpopular third shift.

"When we started working the job, I realized I was just incredibly arrogant," admits Bartley. "Before that, I just never put myself in the shoes of someone who might be working a cash register—at night. And all of a sudden I realized, the line that separates an executive from somebody who's working a cash register is a very, very thin one."

"Honestly, being in that position is very humbling," agrees Lueck, now earning $55,000 doing contract work within IT once more. Both men quickly gained a new and powerful appreciation for their ability to leave retail behind—as they both did—and return to the white-collar professional world they knew and loved.

Knowing, or feeling fairly certain, your former field or industry will eventually welcome you back, with its reassuringly middle- or upper-middle-class perks of healthy pay, paid vacations and sick days, highly educated colleagues, and opportunities for advancement creates a bright line between those who work retail for a while, appreciating its refuge while they regroup, and those who find their former lives impossible to reclaim. All the while I worked at The North Face, I was still writing and editing, being well paid to produce work for national publications like *The New York Times* and *Smithsonian*. I still had a handhold on my former identity. I was lucky in this respect. Many fields don't allow for a freelance banker, teacher, or nurse. You either have a job—a good job you really want—or you don't.

For those U6ers with few other choices, retail's sharply delineated tasks and pay feel less like a safety net than a noose. They now find themselves trapped in a world they find depressing, lonely, and dull.

As I did at The North Face, both men wore a uniform in their retail jobs—a green apron and a blue polo shirt—and had to shift their brains into neutral. No longer were they flying around the world to meetings or strategizing with peers, but instead spent their shift stocking shelves with candy, gum, energy drinks, reading glasses, and batteries, moving products from back to front to present customers with a tidy, attractive presentation.

Not knowing when or if they would escape their $8-per-hour grind was tough. "While looking for work and doing this work, it was a roller coaster," Lueck says. "I would have an interview and think I have a good chance at getting a new job, but it wouldn't work out. The longer I was there, it was very hard. I don't *want* to work at night!"

For Sarah McFarlane, a fifty-one-year-old mother of four working part-time as an associate for Williams-Sonoma, a national upscale chain of cookware stores, retail initially looked like a good bet. Her last full-time job, fifteen years earlier, had been as a systems analyst for a major insurance firm. Now she makes $10 an hour, with no commission. She, too, just needed a steady income.

As many newcomers do, she began working during the holidays, between Thanksgiving Day and Christmas, hoping to be hired into a regular part-time position afterward. She liked the employee discount and splurged, for a while.

It was a huge adjustment from her previous professional job, as much for the low pay as for the physical exhaustion of working on her feet all day long, even to the point where she needed to wear shoes with arch supports.

Eager to do her new job well, she expected—but never received—formal training.

"The trouble is, people come into our store and expect service and expect us to be experts. We have a gazillion products and get new ones in all the time. People think we have used or tried everything, and that is not humanly possible. I look like an idiot when a customer wants to know how a new garlic gadget works and I have trouble showing him. During slow times we are supposed to read the boxes/signs so we know more about the products."

(At The North Face, at least, we all received ongoing quarterly training, both online through a computer multiple-choice quiz that we had to complete successfully and within a set amount of time and with detailed, printed tests. Everyone had to do them. Whether we enjoyed it was a moot point, but it did guarantee we had up-to-date product knowledge as new merchandise arrived each season.)

McFarlane's shoppers, like ours, are wealthy and spoiled.

"Many, many times I'm talking to a customer and another one comes up and interrupts, 'Can you help me find . . . ?', 'Do you have . . . ?', 'I need . . .' Don't they see that I'm helping someone else?"

By April 2010, during our final conversations, McFarlane was working three part-time jobs in an effort to boost her income, and she was fed up. "I need a satisfying job where I am compensated for what I am worth and treated with respect."

She's also worn out by the sobering, large gap between her fantasy of retail, certainly for a nationally known and prestigious brand like Willams-Sonoma, and its dull daily reality. "I was extremely surprised at how little employees mattered and how inefficiently things are run. It's all about the sale."

Beth Fults, thirty-nine, worked in Minneapolis for six years as an architect before moving to Aspen—where she now sells ski clothing for a living. After six years in her chosen field, she was laid off in 2008. She sought another job, but after many long months sending her résumé to several states—and receiving no reply—she was getting desperate. She had never before worked in retail, but it looked like her best option.

"I was a little worried, since I knew nothing about selling ski wear and would be working on commission. I was used to a straight salary and being able to budget from week to week and month to month."

It was an adjustment, professionally, physically, and financially. Fults now earns $7.50 an hour plus a 3 percent commission. "I don't like the lack of a consistent paycheck. It's tough to budget when your check fluctuates every week." She has also had to forgo another perk of a salaried job: paid vacation days.

"I've had to drastically downsize to make ends meet," she admits. "More roommates, smaller place, less going out and on vacations. After I've done all that, I'm able to get the bills paid and slowly pay off credit cards. I was living off my credit cards when I first got laid off, so I have a long ways to go to get those paid off."

Like others who stay on the sales floor for a while, she's become accustomed to it.

"It's come to the point now that I actually enjoy most days and look forward to seeing friends when they are out skiing. For the most part, customers are very pleasant and really ask questions and seek us out. Most value our product knowledge and experience.

"I actually don't mind working in retail. They promoted me and gave me a bit of a raise after the first year and I work the days my manager has off. I really like seeing the new products every year and 'shopping' with the guests when they are excited about their new purchases. The thing I like least about it is the competitiveness with the other salespeople and the cattiness that can come of it. Everyone eventually settles in, but for the first month or two of the season it can be very competitive."

One of the toughest challenges for previously well-educated or high-earning workers is retail's attendant loss of professional identity and status. Having a network of people who applaud you for gutting it out helps, says Fults. "My friends—and especially my family—are proud of my independence, that I'm able to support myself and branch out. I'm not ashamed to accept a job that's not in my original long-term plan. They just admire my willingness to work."

My own family and friends were just as supportive, even as a few wondered why I wasn't as successful selling my freelance work as I was pushing T-shirts and jackets. No one, not even my friends who had won some of the highest honors in journalism, found my retail decision strange—if I needed to earn some extra cash, that was my decision and they respected it. Fellow freelancers, many of them feeling the same pinch as I was, were sympathetic; I knew of three, all middle-aged women, also working part-time retail jobs themselves.

A few fellow journalists still employed full-time in our field watched my trajectory with the horrified gaze of the unscathed. They had seen twenty-four thousand print journalists nationwide lose their jobs in one year and any of them could soon be next. Like me, anyone over forty-five earning a decent wage was most likely to feel the ax, quickly replaced by two cheaper and more pliable twenty-five-year-olds. They gratefully admitted they now better appreciated their own jobs, no matter how harried. There but for the grace of God . . . They at least weren't wearing a plastic badge doing mindless, repetitive tasks. They, still, didn't have to try anything so unfamiliar, low-status, or boring.

"I could never do it!" admitted one with a shudder. "Good for you."

The nights I staggered home after a busy shift, showered off the sweat, and fell into bed, Jose greeted me with a fierce hug. His family had not grown up with money, his father a small-town preacher, his mother a kindergarten teacher. More than anyone in my life—and a fellow career journalist—he also knew and valued not only my hard work and the income I brought into our household as a result, but what a change this was from every other job I'd had. My feet aflame with exhaustion, I shifted restlessly for hours in pain every Tuesday night—and after every additional shift I worked in the holidays. I couldn't believe how much my feet hurt, and couldn't imagine the stamina it took to work that job full-time.

"I'm really proud of you," he'd whisper. "You're doing it. I admire you so much for doing what we need right now." His respect gave me a dignity I needed.

Fults, Bartley, Lueck, and McFarlane all made their peace with retail, able to accept it as a source of income and relish some pleasure within it. Not Cynthia Norton, fifty-two, a former administrative assistant in Jacksonville, Florida. For her, working retail is an unwanted dead end, a place where she feels stuck—now earning a third of her former income.

She loved her administrative assistant work and enjoyed her income. She started work as an assistant for her aunt at sixteen but after decades in her field was laid off in 2008 and hasn't found another job using those skills. Norton has sent out hundreds of résumés without luck. Twice, job openings she interviewed for were eliminated, one shortly after she started work.

Norton was featured in a *New York Times* story on the "new poor," those unable to find anything more than low-wage work even after months or years of searching. This group—comprising generally older workers—has pulled up the average length of time that a current worker has been unemployed to a record high of thirty-three weeks as of April 2010. "The percentage of unemployed people who have been looking for jobs for more than six months is at 45.9 percent, the highest in at least six decades," the paper reported.

Workers like her are falling far and fast, some—through their drastically reduced incomes—plunging, single and terrified, out of the middle class and into the miserable ranks of the working poor. By the summer of 2010, though, as the recession dragged on, the U6ers had been supplanted by a newer, even more frightened group, the 99ers, people who had exhausted their federally extended ninety-nine weeks of unemployment benefits but still had not been able to find work.

Not only does this downward spiral, the American dream reversed, hit our pocketbooks. It's destroying our spirits. Norton, who has spent most of the last two years working part-time at Walmart as a cashier, told the *Times*, "A monkey could do what I do," of her work as a cashier. "Actually, a monkey would get bored." (In June 2009, I wrote these exact, furious words to myself.)

If you've grown accustomed to any sort of intellectual challenge in your work, you can *feel* your brain atrophy after a few years in low-level retail. Ask Nancy Schwarz, a fifty-one-year-old working in Raleigh, North Carolina, for Belk, a regional department store. Drowning in $40,000 of educational debt from acquiring a master's degree in non-profit management and $20,000 more in credit card debt, she sees no escape from the retail ghetto.

Not while earning $7.25 an hour as a sales associate.

To make ends meet, to her deep frustration and shame, she receives additional funds every month from her mother, who is eighty-one. She started working for Belk in November 2009 after working for a local florist whom she'd had to convince to hire her.

Schwarz has become bitter and angry, having fallen a long, long way from middle-class life and its comforts. Every day reminds her that all those years of experience and education—her last staff job was with Habitat For Humanity's headquarters in Americus, Georgia—are, for now, worthless.

She was laid off from Habitat with one month's notice in 2007 and discovered she couldn't collect unemployment benefits, not uncommon in the world of nonprofits but a terrible shock to a single woman with no savings or other means of support. "I was ignorant. I didn't know they weren't paying into it for me." Feeling betrayed by an organization widely admired for its mission of helping others, Schwarz now sees the world differently. "I don't make assumptions about anything."

Like Norton, she loved her old job, even at the relatively low salary of $35,000, and took enormous pride in it. *She had chosen it.* Unlike retail's deadening, dead-end life, her Habitat work satisfied her intellectually, emotionally, and spiritually. It also offered serious perks, like world travel and interesting colleagues.

Schwarz's work made a significant difference in others' lives, an emotional satisfaction that offset her low wages. Not now. She's angry at her wasted skill, her huge investment in a degree that isn't working for her, and feels lonely, isolated from other professional-level workers with similar advanced education or backgrounds or interests. She hates the daily disconnect between her ideas, skills, idealism—and the minimal demands of her retail job.

"They don't care what I bring to this work. They just want results. I'm very, very disappointed. I've never had this much interaction with this part of society. I don't like it! I don't want to be a part of it! It's not who I am."

It is also deeply unpleasant, if you once earned enough income to enjoy small luxuries, to witness the fawning attention stores lavish on shoppers at the literal expense of the workers there serving them. The money that stores devote to their labor budgets—between 8 and 13 percent—is almost always the absolute least. It's contemptuous, and expecting a cheery corporate demeanor in response only salts the wound. It cost The North Face thousands to send their sponsored athletes to China or Tibet or India, where they were photographed for the lavish images in our stores. I calculated that cost and wondered how many customers, if any, ever even noticed these pictures. I doubt any of them realized these were sponsored athletes whose bravery and adventurous spirit were meant to inspire them to equal heights—not just random models.

Did they even care?

Schwarz, too, hates watching her company spend lavishly on events designed to bring in wealthy local women shoppers—in the case of Belk, with a band, food, and wine "that must cost hundreds of thousands of dollars"—while paying her such paltry wages. "It's demoralizing and degrading. It can do a real number on your self-esteem. What I've had to do is humble myself and live in the moment. I can't think about doing this next month or the month after that.

"I can't even *think* about next year."

Like Cynthia Norton, Schwarz feels like she's in free fall, watching the world whiz past her in a dizzying, disorienting blur. "I really don't see this recession ending anytime soon. I think there's going to be a huge shift in how people work. *What are we going to do?* I don't *want* to learn a new skill. I don't want to work in high-tech. Why should I?"

Retail work's toughest adjustment, then, from a professional office job with a title or perks or highly educated coworkers, isn't simply the loss of income, status, or the realistic hope of earning a promotion. All of these are difficult and depressing enough to forgo, *if they're temporary*. Retail can provide a safety net, but it's not a place where anyone with ambition wants to stay. Or can afford to.

Work defines many of us. It offers us our identity. For a woman, especially, who is single and has no children, it can be our primary, core source of self-worth. A steady middle-class income is also—especially crucial for women, who live longer than men and often outlive their husbands, if they are married—the only way to ensure a decent old age, by making enough money to save enough for a dignified retirement, not simply spinning the hamster wheel of low-wage labor.

Take away decently compensated employment that matters to us, and our souls begin to die.

* * *

As the recession tightened its grip through the spring of 2009, I felt safe, if only for one night a week, in The North Face's brightly lit space. No matter how bored or annoyed I got, and I did, it still offered me a secure port in the economic storm that had, in the past six months, become a howling, terrifying Category 5 hurricane. I looked forward to the certainty of diversion, of straightforward tasks I knew how to do, friendly coworkers, and managers who knew and liked and trusted me. Even our unspeakable Muzak had improved. One night, eating dinner in the food court, I heard a sound so disorienting it took me a minute to place it—the Salvation Army's fund-raising bells, being rung midsummer, in July 2009. For the first time ever, their constituents were so needy they simply couldn't wait until Christmas.

I was learning a lot in this job. Not, unfortunately, about retail's intricacies—how merchandise is designed or sourced or shipped or priced. We would never be privy to anything that substantive. But, every Tuesday night, putting on my red and white plastic badge and stepping onto the sales floor offered me a paid tutorial in human nature. Theirs and mine.

"We rely on good jobs for our sense of well-being," writes therapist and *Listening to Prozac* author Peter D. Kramer in *The Wall Street Journal*. "Increasingly, it's the workplace, as much as the home, that provides lessons about how to face personal challenges . . . When [the workplace] functions well, it teaches all of us when to stand our ground and when to be strategic . . . Confronting what we work in, we discover our strengths, and we learn humility . . . Good jobs strengthen identity."

I saw this in spades.

I had never realized quite so clearly why I had enjoyed journalism. I like writing and exploring new subjects. I love telling stories. But I *really* enjoy meeting and talking with a wide array of people. Working retail reinforced this for me with a new clarity because its primary demands forced me to focus on others' needs, not just listening to them in order to express their ideas or explain their positions on an issue. I had never before stepped away from journalism, so had never had a chance to miss it or to acquire new skills unrelated to that field. Now I also saw that some of the skills I'd spent thirty years perfecting might translate to other forms of paid work.

Rewarded only for those behaviors that suited my journalism bosses—get in first, get the quote fast, get out—I'd become lopsided and out of balance, like a dancer working only one side of her body or a lifter strengthening only his legs. I'd focused for decades, since college, primarily on my intellectual abilities, the ones on which I had always prided myself.

This new job demanded a more sophisticated emotional intelligence, finally and belatedly forcing me to up my game in relating well to others, not simply taking notes and fleeing back to a newsroom full of cynics.

Journalism rewards behaviors that in most other fields are derided as antisocial and obnoxious: do whatever it takes to get a story first, then crow loudly so that everyone can admire you and your employer. Bang on private doors and stick cameras in people's faces and shriek, "How do you feel?" at grieving relatives.

To succeed as a journalist meant leashing your kinder, gentler qualities, if you had any, freeing them only when useful for nailing an interview or source. Much as I loved the intellectual challenges of journalism, I rarely liked or socialized with colleagues I too often found cold, hard, selfish, and ruthlessly ambitious. Being surrounded by people behaving badly brought out the worst in my own highly competitive character. I wondered when, where, or if my better qualities—my playful humor, my compassion, and my joy in sincerely connecting with others—would ever find expression within a job.

Here in retail, finally, they had.

On the sales floor, I encountered dozens of strangers every week, from surgeons to jet pilots, Chileans to Finns, an impoverished senior with chipped nail polish to a preppy blonde headed back to Harvard. I was getting paid to hear their stories and put them at ease. These were skills I'd developed through decades of working in journalism, but too often, now, working in journalism felt like a losing battle: editors were cutting their story assignments and budgets and people I contacted for interviews were often wary.

Civilians, the nonprepped, often don't trust us journalists, or they think, with good reason, we'll twist their words or images to our own ends.

Public figures—and I had interviewed CEOs and prime ministers and celebrities—typically arrived swaddled in pomposity, a flack ensuring that my questions remained inbounds and my interviewee stayed on message. The fear I'd misquote these public figures neutered too many interviews.

On the sales floor, though, I wasn't threatening at all. I was there to serve, to help, to make life easier. So shoppers, the pleasant ones, often responded to me with gratitude and appreciation. It's an easy, quick high knowing you can make someone happy within minutes. A good associate can do that. It's addictive. Who doesn't like knowing they've been useful?

I really appreciated, for once, being appreciated. Like this letter, sent to me and my managers, by a female customer my age:

> All too often employers hear only a customer's negative comments. I am writing to praise the service provided to my daughter and me this week . . .
>
> Having two daughters, 21 and 17, I have to shop more than I might like, especially for stylish, "warm" items, since my eldest attends university in upstate New York, where temperatures get quite cold.
>
> Upon entry [to your store] we were warmly greeted by Caitlin Kelly who knew exactly where the jacket [we sought] was located. Delighted that a salesperson actually knew what and where the item was, I was satisfied, and proceeded to have my daughter try on both the x-small and the small. Caitlin continued to impress us when she came back to see how we were doing, and helped us discuss the merits of each size. Caitlin possessed a knowledge of the cut and styling of that jacket,

as well as [two others] which my daughter already has. She was charming and knowledgeable, and able to relate to both my daughter and to me. She made shopping [in your store] a pleasure, and I felt you should know what a treasure you have in Caitlin. Every store should have such exceptional representation.

I enjoyed knowing our products well enough to surprise shoppers like her, who had been jaded by incompetent service. Or I'd switch into fluent French or decent Spanish when necessary. When I met customers heading to Fiji or Tanzania or Costa Rica or Cuzco, I offered them enthusiastic practical advice, whether on malaria medications or riptides, because I had been to all of these places. I loved sharing their excitement and anticipation, while my street cred as someone who had been there and done that lent my words—and my resulting sales—authority. This job, and our endlessly diverse customers, required skills I'd had for years, but had never been able to combine professionally: linguist, travel agent, athlete, survivor of sports-related surgery and physical therapy—and empathetic salesperson.

We had customers from all over the world, including a few unlikely spots I had visited, from the tiny Breton town of Concarneau to Galway City. It gave us something in common, an easy starting point for conversation, trust, and pleasure. I don't know how people sell well without that.

Many, even during a brief chat, shared cool arcana: a female graduate student of neuroscience, in a wheelchair, told me how intelligent octopi are; a couple from Iceland, both of whom had lost their jobs, described firsthand that nation's fiscal breakdown; a senior executive from a beer company (we knew someone in common) traded notes with me on management styles.

As in journalism, everyone had a story.

I had never before found it easy to make small talk and often had been misread, as a result, as unfriendly and prickly. Mostly, like many writers who focus our attention away from ourselves and onto our subjects, I was really more shy and private. Selling—and having to move $1,500 to $6,000 worth of merchandise off the floor each shift within seven hours—leaves no room for reticence. This job was teaching me, however belatedly, that a simple, sincere, friendly greeting *could* forge a connection.

But selling well is a delicate dance, a seduction. After our initial basic training, where we took turns doing a few hours of role-playing, we were all on our own. Unlike some companies—like Japanese apparel giant Uniqlo, which insists its associates use six key phrases to sell—we had no set script. As long as we did sell, we were fine. That autonomy, when so much else in our work was videotaped and dissected and quantified, was essential to my enjoyment of the job. I never would have stayed without it.

Every shift offered lessons in another life skill: coping with the unexpected. We never knew who or how many would walk through our doors, or in what mood, or what they might be seeking. And, unlike in journalism, I gratefully experienced forgiveness. We weren't punished for falling short of our sales goals; if you're standing around an empty store, there's no one to sell *to*.

Selling is one-on-one, a sort of private conversation that, when done well, finishes with a transaction at the cash wrap. It was all up to me to make that happen and I looked forward each week to that individual challenge. I knew that every encounter, no matter how fleeting, left an impression on our shoppers. They might not buy anything that night, that month, or even that year. That was okay. *They needed to feel comfortable.* Sometimes, as I do myself, they were just doing recon for a gift or for when they got a new job or a raise or a bonus.

Unlike my writing—read and judged by millions after I had competed for jobs or assignments, each word read and revised and questioned by multiple editors—my sales job was deeply, powerfully, endorphin-pumpingly personal. I watched my customers carefully, silently stalking them, observing their haste or languor, their body language, clothing, jewelry, grooming, confidence. You could tell who was happy and who was itching for a fight. It was my job to initiate the sale, keep it going, ensure that it didn't derail or explode halfway through. I learned to suss out the tire-kickers and fussbudgets, people for whom nothing was ever quite right. You could waste an hour on them, and we sometimes did.

Every new encounter offered me a fresh chance to create, and enjoy, a momentary intimacy with my customers. I loved it. "Be my wife, will ya?" joked one man, searching for a jacket that fit well. "Happy to!" I joked back. I loved putting strangers at ease, calming them down, making their brief time with me—when possible—a fun, playful, interesting part of their day. And mine.

One holiday-season afternoon, a man in his thirties came in with his wife and began pawing impatiently through a rack of men's jackets. He was barely looking at them, he was so agitated. He and his wife were beautifully dressed—he in a crisp tattersall shirt, she wearing large diamond studs. Our prices weren't the problem.

"Can I help?" I asked.

He appeared on the verge of tears. "I need to find a present for *a pain in the ass!*"

"I have a few of those in my own family. No problem," I replied. "So, what size is this pain in the ass? What colors does he like?"

His angst was safe with me. We'd figure it out.

What an irony. People like him *had it made.* He probably earned a fortune, owned a mansion or two, maybe ran a hedge fund or oversaw a budget worth millions. But one nasty relative had scared him so badly he needed me—the $11-per-hour clerk—to help him out. This wasn't the sort of thing they taught at Harvard Business School. I felt like a superhero, able to leap mile-high neuroses in a single bound. I could do something, quickly and easily, that he couldn't. And I could help reduce his anxiety. It felt really good.

His shoulders dropped with relief. He bought several items and returned an hour later to buy even more.

I now understood why the words "retail" and "therapy" fit so well together. So many emotions! So much drama! People buying holiday gifts practically vibrated with fear, as though making a misguided but loving choice—offering someone the wrong brand, color, style, or size—might prove somehow fatal. It didn't help when, typically, they had no idea of the recipients' sizes or colors or what they owned—even when it was their own teenage daughter.

It escalated to hysteria as each Christmas Eve drew closer. Joe and I raised an eyebrow at one another across the floor and shared a smile.

"I hate the holidays," he said.

* * *

Selling clothing—unlike hardware or cars or CDs—often means touching someone's body as they try on a garment or footwear, both emotionally and physically intimate. Some people, I know, are wary of a stranger's touch, so I'd always ask first. Many times, they'd request my advice on a size or style or color, which requires trust. Just as we summed shoppers up within seconds, so did they with us—deciding, quickly, if they actually wanted us help them. Most of The North Face's clothing fits tightly, which meant that many women were too curvy, or fat, to wear them. I lost track of the number of times I commiserated with them, sincerely, then a size 16 myself, as they tugged and pulled fruitlessly at an unforgiving garment.

"It's not you!" I'd laugh, kindly. "We have breasts and hips, and these clothes are cut for skinny teenagers." They'd sigh, grateful for my empathy. Those emotional connections, and the skill I brought to them, never showed in our sales statistics and so never won me, or others, recognition or praise. Those moments—for me—were the pleasure of working retail. Simply moving merch was a mechanical exercise.

Our team, in general, also enjoyed a growing affection for one another. Not everyone got along, of course, but when Jared—a young, funny former colleague who had left the year before to work for a competing store nearby—came back at Christmas 2009 to help out, he was greeted with delighted hugs. We had someone back we knew and liked, who would lighten not only our collective workload, but our mood at the toughest season of the year.

Retail's long hours and shift work can strain even the best relationships. Angela, discovering she was not only pregnant but that the baby, her first, was due right around Black Friday—the single busiest day of the retail calendar as it kicks off huge holiday sales—had to keep working. *On her feet.* Already about ten to fifteen pounds overweight, Angie had suffered for years from persistent and debilitating lower back pain. I'd urged her to see a physician, as her salaried position included health insurance, but now it was too late to take any time off and I often saw her wincing in pain as she leaned over the counter or crossed the sales floor.

We liked Angie, and appreciated her soft-spoken role as intermediary between Joe, who was often pretty gruff with some of my colleagues, and the rest of us. Being pregnant in her role as assistant manager was rough on her; one of her nightly tasks as a "keyholder" was to kneel at the store's huge, heavy sliding glass front door and lock it shut into the floor. One night she simply forgot, potentially leaving the store vulnerable to thieves. Nothing happened, but it made clear that a bulging belly and a job on your feet all day are not a great combination.

A month before she was due, Angie was diagnosed with high blood pressure and put on bed rest, pushing her out of our team a month earlier than planned. She was ready for a break, as she said with a sigh to me one afternoon: "They want the world." It wasn't clear if she meant the company or our customers. Both were insatiable.

We wanted to throw a baby shower for her. Several of my coworkers, already parents, conferred on what she might need or want. The problem?

We all worked totally different shifts and couldn't, ever, find a time or place convenient to all of us, to give her a card and some gifts and celebrate. Those who worked Saturday, and clocked out by nine forty-five p.m. after a long, wearying day were in no mood to party much later—many of them still facing another one to two hours' travel by public transit to get home—especially if they had to be back in the store the next morning by noon. I finally just brought her a card and a gift, a New Mom To-Do List with gag suggestions.

Our small team, like many in the recession as more educated and professional workers filled the ranks, offered a wide range of personalities, work ethics, and ideals, which sometimes made it a challenge for us to work well as a unit. Some were just lazy. Some took shortcuts—one spent hours meticulously and visibly "sleeving" the hundreds of jackets on display, making sure that their knife edges were perfectly aligned. What he *hadn't* done, which was even more important and also required, was to sort every single one of them into size order. That meant going back through every single row he had just touched—including re-doing the damn sleeving! Some spent hours texting or phoning their friends and family or taking smoking breaks while the rest of us did our jobs.

I admit it—I dodged one task: cleaning the bathroom. I cleaned the rest of the store more than almost anyone, and was perfectly happy to do so, with Windex and paper towel, a mop or broom. But I wasn't going to scrub the damn toilet, even after, in my 2008 formal written review, I was told to. No one, thank God, ever pushed me on it, guessing, perhaps, I might quit over that issue.

Tam hated this demand as well. "I ain't cleaning no toilets!" she agreed. But she did. As a full-timer she couldn't be as invisible as me. I found it a disgusting task. Only half our staff was female, so the seat was usually left up and God knows what the floor and bowl would be like. The job was already rife with humiliation and grinding physical labor. Now this?

For whatever reason, none of my coworkers ever confronted me about this failing. If they gossiped about me behind my back, it would be news to me.

I didn't think I was better than anyone or above such tasks in general. I happily clean my own toilet at home. I just didn't want to do it for a company that kept cheaping us out. I consistently sold a lot of merchandise, never called in sick and clocked in on time. Fairly or not, I counted on that track record for some leeway. We all knew we screwed the pooch, just in different ways; some sat on the toilet for twenty minutes texting; others disappeared to buy a soft drink or to smoke; one or two sat on the stockroom's lone folding chair and just took a desperately needed, and never-offered, brief break.

Some of us faced thwarted professional ambitions, including those with alleged felony convictions that made getting any good job difficult—and which made moving up in retail, and thereby being responsible for our cash registers, impossible. This job was, de facto, a dead end one for them. The best they might hope for was some steady income for a while and a good, maybe great, reference from Joe. Some people's plans, even in their thirties, remained vague or unformed. Others were on hold, for now or forever. Carl, studying psychology at community college, loved school and said he planned to keep studying for many more years, maybe all the way to a doctorate. But even he, a lover of academia, was cynical enough that, as we shared our possible next steps, he wondered aloud what those might actually be.

The plaintive, standard refrain of the underemployed—"But I have a college degree!"—impressed no one, Carl least of all.

"We've all got degrees," he would say with a rueful smile.

Whether we'd stayed in the wrong, shrinking industry for too long—my case, perhaps—or had never developed sufficiently strong interviewing or people skills, hadn't built up networks on LinkedIn, or acquired a graduate degree or specialized industry knowledge, we were all stuck, whether for now or for good. Retail had its own brand of intimacy in this respect; for many of us, it was a holding tank. Like fish deeply weary of the same little castle and an artificial sea bottom of colored pebbles—but without a larger pond to jump into—we'd swim restlessly around our tank week after week, month after month, wondering what, if anything, was our next move.

Several of our male associates were taking exams to become a cop or a court officer, secure government jobs with pensions, the latter paying about $50,000 to start. That, we knew, beat retail unless they got a store manager's spot. And, in our store anyway, I saw little passion for retail.

Even our salaried managers, Angie and Joe, who at least had good pay, benefits, and the chance of promotions or raises, looked weary, beleaguered, and overwhelmed. Both were smart and hardworking, but the demands from corporate were relentless. They spent much of their days on the phone in conference calls or staring at a computer screen, not managing or coaching us or working with customers. They had more to lose—a decent income with benefits in a vicious recession—and lived in a kind of fear that we witnessed with some sympathy but little desire to experience firsthand. Every few weeks a regional or district manager would descend to inspect the premises and our displays, sending us into a frenzy of floor-scrubbing and tag-tucking. Everything had to be perfect. If it wasn't a senior manager coming in to find fault—they rarely found anything positive to say—it was the regular, spontaneous visits by "secret shoppers." We were issued, like many working in retail who forever live in fear of the next surprise visit by these faceless inspectors, a detailed multipage checklist of behaviors we had to follow without hesitation or deviation. If we failed a secret shop (which was easy to do and which we did a few times), we'd all lose shared bonuses, no matter how high our sales.

The corporate mind-set was punitive, escalating, demanding. It felt medieval, the serfs rushing to tug their forelocks when the district manager or his boss or—only once—*his* boss occasionally galloped into town.

We only knew the names of guys two levels up. I never even knew the name of our company's CEO. Like the rest of our crew, I didn't really care.

What mattered, to all of us, was what happened in *our* store. Since I knew what the more senior of the two managers looked like, I killed him with kindness when he arrived at our store for the first time, to Joe's relief.

We also saw what this constant stress did to our managers, Angie and Joe, two pretty mellow people. Given the effect it was having on them, who *would* want to become a store manager or assistant?

Our own bonuses were a slap in the face. Only after selling $30,000 worth of merchandise (which took me about a year, each time,) would we get a gift card—for the company's products—worth $25.

There was nowhere to rise within this company, at least not locally. Zeke, the merchandiser, had moved to California with his wife to do the same job there for the same company. But most of my coworkers, including me, had wives or husbands or life partners and/or family in this region. No one wanted to simply uproot and move far away . . . for what?

In the recession, there were no jobs anyway.

Over a pile of T-shirts, folding together being one of the few chances we had to chat privately, I once asked Tameisha directly, "What's your exit strategy? Do you plan to get out of retail?" She said yes, once her son, now four, was in school full-time. But she had no specific goal in mind. Escaping, and climbing the ladder into something more promising, often felt overwhelming and difficult.

And Tam, to her dismay, was being pressured by her friends and neighbors to have a second child. As a single mother. For about six months, she had, in our time together, a nice boyfriend with a decent, steady white-collar job, but she had eventually dumped him. Not ambitious enough, she said.

"I can barely support the baby I already have!" she said, clearly exasperated by the expectation that she'd take this popular route. Her friends, she told me, wanted her to be more like them, have a couple of kids. If that meant staying in poverty, certainly in a low-wage job with no room to move up, and, likely of necessity, in public housing as well, so be it. Proud, ambitious, and educated, Tam found these low expectations horrifying. It sometimes felt like she looked to me—a woman almost twice her age who had had some decent jobs along the way—for moral support.

I was 100 percent behind her on this one and told her so, plainly. Another child without a second income would only postpone her ability to flee the ghetto of retail, and we both knew it.

Determination to better her situation, professionally and personally, was Tam's fuel source: to get out of debt (which she did), to get her own apartment (which she did), and, once she got it, to make sure it was exactly to her liking, down to the color and style and size of her window blinds. I had been to Paris while working at the store—a fiftieth birthday gift from my fiancé, Jose—and I had created a small book of images I'd shot there, in color, black-and-white, and sepia. I wanted to give Tam a housewarming gift and asked if she'd like one of the photos. She chose an eleven-by-fourteen sepia image of a Bateaux-Mouches boat on the Seine at sunset. I would never see it on her wall, but that wasn't the point. I wanted her, a woman I liked and admired, someone who values elegance and style, to enjoy something beautiful.

Tam and I had a few unlikely things in common, which we discovered over years working the same shift. We had both been badly bullied in high school—she for her dark skin, me for being too outspoken. As a result, both of us had developed sharp tongues, always at the ready with a nasty quip. Our banter was often so sharp-edged people gasped, but we were like two baby tigers swatting one another in play, having learned young how to verbally defend ourselves. We also both had fathers who had been emotionally and/or physically absent much of the time, and stepsiblings we barely knew or had never met. She and I talked about all the things women who spend a lot of time together end up discussing— our families, our friendships, whether to wax or pluck our facial hair, what birth control we'd tried and liked.

And we were both working hard to clear a pile of credit card debt.

Our friendship, albeit limited to our time in the store, involved plenty of teasing. "You know, you ain't wrapped too tight!" she'd exclaim on nights I was acting silly to let off steam, but she said it with an indulgent smile. For our second Christmas, I gave her a bottle of deep silver nail polish I'd spotted at Sephora. "It had your name on it, baby," I told her—Queen of Everything.

Over the years working together, we at the store met each other's husbands and wives, partners and children. Peter's second child, another daughter, was born in November 2009 and, although her mom brought her in only three months later, we all saw her within days—in the photos on Carl's cell phone. While I never became close enough to anyone there to spend time with them beyond those walls, others clearly did. Whether it was due to race or age or having a few young kids, they all had more in common with one another than I did with each of them.

When Joe fell head over heels for a new woman, we teased him affectionately about his hasty decision to add another tattoo, of her name, inside his left wrist. One night Janelle, a college student with whom I'd barely spoken, was folding T-shirts with me. Usually loud and lively, she seemed subdued and I asked why. She poured her heart out to me: her boyfriend had dumped her. I was surprised she wanted to tell me about it, but I listened sympathetically. I'd had my heart shattered plenty of times, and remembered what it felt like at twenty-one. At one of our meetings, Shaniqua brought in her youngest, now nineteen months, in a dinosaur-print onesie. We realized with a jolt of surprise how long we had known one another—that this was the baby she had been newly pregnant with when we were hired in September 2007.

I tried twice to invite several of my coworkers to my home, but was rebuffed both times. I own an apartment in a simple sixty-year-old, red-brick building with an outdoor pool. It's a real refuge on steamy summer days and I invited several women to come by and enjoy it. They preferred to head to the beach.

"Ooooh. A *pool!* How fancy!" said Tam.

Her words, and sarcastic tone, stung.

After a few minutes, she added quietly, "I don't know how to swim."

"Neither does Jose!" I reassured her. "I figure you'd just come by and look decorative if you wanted."

But it was clear she had no interest and I never asked again.

On a few occasions, it became clear that I and some of my coworkers experienced life very differently.

One afternoon, when Angie was newly pregnant, Joe casually announced that Frank, her boyfriend, had been stabbed.

Stabbed?

Apparently he'd gotten into a bar fight but wasn't seriously injured.

"You know Jorge got stabbed?" Joe added.

"Jorge got stabbed?" We sounded like a Marx Brothers routine.

"Some girl stabbed him in the back. He wouldn't go to the hospital. He staggered in for work one Sunday morning and we wondered why he was walking funny."

"Bill got stabbed, too," Joe added conversationally.

"You're *kidding*, right? Where? How?"

"No. In his arm. His wife did it."

This was a first. What's the etiquette when inquiring—or do you?—about a stabbing? I still had never found out how, why, or even *whether* several of my coworkers had criminal records, as had been rumored. There was no one to ask if the rumors were true, and it wasn't the kind of thing that just naturally came up in conversation, like where we went to high school.

But Bill I knew well enough.

"So, I hear you got stabbed," I said on the floor.

"Yeah," he said calmly, a little sheepishly.

"Where?" I asked. He showed me a large scar on his left bicep.

Bill was one of the softest-spoken men I'd ever met. Confrontation, conflict, a raised voice were simply not his style.

"You must have *really* pissed her off. That must have bled like a son of a bitch! Did the police come?"

"Yeah," he said.

She had not been arrested; the mother of their four kids stayed with him. Or vice versa.

Joe and I tried to make sense of this, but failed. It wasn't a value judgment, but this wasn't our world.

"I've never managed a store with so many stabbings," he said. "Tell you one thing I've learned—never date a woman south of Yonkers. They'll cut you!"

One evening I sat for about an hour in the tiny office with Carl. We'd never spoken at length, although we'd always gotten along well. He was a guy, a black man, a college student, much younger than I, passionate about his motorcycle. We didn't have a lot in common to talk about. But he'd been complaining for weeks about his long-distance girlfriend. It felt like he wanted to talk about it with me, and I was happy to listen.

"She's always pushing me to stand up for her," he said. "We go out in public, to a bar, and she'll get hit on by some guy and then wait for me to step in and tell him to back off."

"She sounds a little insecure. What's the harm in doing it? Sounds like she's looking to you for reassurance."

He looked at me and paused, perhaps measuring how much to tell me—and how much I could handle. "A friend of mine got shot in the head for doing that," he said quietly.

In mid-November 2009, I overheard Jorge and Rafael, our twenty-five-year-old stock clerk, talking excitedly about a big party they were attending together that weekend. They planned to dress up, as the party invitation specified, in "Real Fancy Style." The card specified no sneakers or boots. The glossy postcard, on both sides, showed color photos of a beautiful young black girl, Fantasia Byrd. It would have been her twenty-first birthday party, the perfect time for all her friends to celebrate.

But the party was a fund-raiser—to buy her grave a headstone and create a reward fund to hunt down her killers. Fantasia, another young retail associate, who grew up in Yonkers where she was close friends with

Jorge and Rafael, had just graduated from community college and moved to Georgia to start fresh. She was killed, at twenty, in Roswell, Georgia, after returning from a party, when a stray bullet through her window hit her in the back of the head. She was playing a board game with her friends at the time.

Retail was a rough little world. But to me and some of my coworkers, it offered a clean, well-lit cocoon.

SEVEN
NEGLECT AND DISRESPECT

One evening, I lost it. Totally decompensated. Went apeshit.

In the main stockroom, where all the clothes were stored, some on racks, some in boxes, I needed a jacket hanging high above my head. It was seven p.m., so the stockroom clerk had gone home. When they were working, these young guys were happy to scramble anywhere necessary with the speed and ease of ironworkers.

Now it was our job to climb up, dig stuff out, and toss or carry it down.

I found one of the store's two shepherd's hooks and extended the light thin pole to a length that might reach. It didn't. The jackets were jammed together so tightly you could barely budge them, and no markers or visible tags on the racks indicated what sizes they were or if the size I needed was even in there. The only way to find out for sure was to clamber up and paw through them.

The stockroom was one of very few places in the store without a security camera. My right shoulder still hurt constantly a year after my surgery and months of physical therapy. And the way these clothes were stacked in the stockroom, forcing anyone my height—five-foot-five—or less to endlessly stretch and reach, was annoying and exhausting.

Why was the company making it so difficult just to do our job?

Was it because all the managers were male—tall and physically powerful? Why didn't the store's designers take shorter employees' difficulties into account? Or the overlords in corporate, who created the store's planogram, the template used to arrange everything on the floor for maximum sales? Didn't anyone in authority notice? Or care?

I'd had it. We were never told why things were so chaotic or why the stock was arranged in ways so consistently dismissive of our need to work comfortably, quickly, and efficiently. In a blind rage, fueled by the sting of the smug corporate assumption we'd just suck it up—or quit, to be quickly replaced by the next drone—I smashed the pole into one of the metal racks, venting my frustration in the only way I could imagine. I felt crazy and stupid trying to achieve excellence while running an obstacle course of obstruction.

And I felt isolated for even *trying* to do my job the best I could.

If my coworkers were equally frustrated, they either quit or said nothing. Our managers clearly didn't care or, if they did, weren't showing it or had no power to make changes. Our district manager, Phil, breezed in and out every few weeks determined to find fault with Joe and with our work—never asking how he might help us do it better.

I had no idea what the pole cost. I didn't care anymore. Clang! Clang! Clang! The fragile ridged metal finally cracked, bent in the middle like a soggy straw.

Shocked by my vandalism, grateful no one had seen it, and deeply ashamed of my tantrum, I hid the evidence of my outburst deep behind some boxes.

I had asked Peter, our prickly sales supervisor, the one I'd had the holiday argument with, why the store's stockrooms were so crowded, disorganized, and poorly designed. Surely he was privy to more information than associates. He had no answer.

The ladder necessary to reach the stockrooms' uppermost shelves and racks was about six feet tall and extremely heavy. It was too heavy for me to drag through the twenty-foot-long stockroom, unfold it, climb it, get stock, climb down, drag it back, reattach it by its bungee cord to the metal shelving—where it blocked access to whatever was behind it—and finally take the desired item out to the sales floor. In more than two years working there, I never saw anyone use it.

Instead, like many of my coworkers, desperate to get stuff quickly to our fussy customers, I'd pull out the folding metal chair—whose bare seat was slippery, and which raised me only seventeen inches and whose grip on the floor was less secure—and strain from that height, cursing every time, to reach whatever I could.

If I couldn't reach it, I couldn't sell it.

"Climbing up onto these chairs is really dangerous!" I fumed aloud to Peter. "Those damn ladders are hopeless. Someone is going to slip and fall one of these days and really hurt themselves."

Peter was so rules-conscious, stuffy and by-the-book in so many ways. Surely he would share my outrage.

"The company has insurance," he replied blandly.

* * *

This attitude, I was starting to see, was typical of our corporate employer, no matter how cordial with us—and he was—our store manager, Joe, remained. If you didn't like it, you could leave. You could, and would, be easily replaced. Employees' safety, productivity, and comfort? Not interested.

Typical of this dismissive attitude was the many months it took to replace the detacher I had broken on Christmas Eve of 2007. It cost $92, and without one at the middle register, whoever worked that central position reached and stretched to use the other two detachers four feet away. Since the device was in a fixed place, we had to accommodate it, not vice versa. That little gesture told us plenty.

If another associate, as was often the case, was folding, sorting, or tagging on the counter between the two registers, that person was in our way and slowing us down. I often wondered if customers noticed how messy and inefficient this was. When things got really crazy and no one had time to keep tidying, the credenza behind us became a messy mountain of bulky, slippery clothing, hats, and gloves. The credenza symbolized everything that was wrong with this job: too much stuff, too few people to move it quickly and tidily, not enough physical space to do our jobs comfortably and efficiently, and, on top of our own frustrations, a shockingly sloppy mess in full view of customers spending hundreds of dollars.

The detacher wasn't replaced for many months, even though our store's sales remained strong. The North Face was still doing just fine financially and easily could have afforded to buy another one. In January of that year, its parent company—the VF Corporation—had $382 million in cash, according to *The Wall Street Journal*.

That they didn't replace the detacher—that Joe and Phil never made this a priority—felt petty, cheap, and demeaning. Like the crowded, crazy-making credenza, it was a daily visible reminder that our only task was to sell a lot of merchandise for as little cost to The North Face as humanly possible. Comfort be damned!

The problem, we started to see, was that Joe had a strictly limited budget for the store and had to work within it. He and his team were controlled by people far away who didn't care about our day-to-day problems, only our sales. How we achieved those sales, and whether problems created by corporate's stingy budgets slowed, hampered, or frustrated those attempts, was of no consequence to them.

This disregard for our needs, forcing us to work without the tools to do our jobs quickly and safely, was clearly normal in retail, since no one else—including veterans of this industry—seemed outraged or indignant. It shocked me. The company was paying a fortune—about what our assistant manager earned *in a year*—each month in rent to the mall. They had clearly invested in a designer and fabricator for the handsome bamboo cabinets and rolling display racks.

But that was all for public eyes. Behind the scenes, behind closed doors, the shoe stockroom was dirty, its structural columns' gray, soft, fluffy insulation shredding off onto our clothing whenever we brushed against it, which was often. It was impossible to reach about 40 percent of the merchandise in either stockroom without a ladder. And even once we'd climbed it, there was no safe, simple way to retrieve the goods; we either carried them down the ladder or threw them onto the floor.

We couldn't even see half the things in there. The Stygian darkness of the shoe stockroom was a design disaster, so poorly lit we could barely read the labels on the boxes. The middle aisle of its three floor-to-ceiling shelves was an inky nightmare. Finally, in desperation at one of our monthly meetings, someone dared to ask for a flashlight, a suggestion Joe dismissed with a laugh.

"The lighting meets code," he said.

With only one or two shepherd's hooks for the entire store—and both stockrooms—we each wasted many valuable minutes every shift trying to find one. Three poles, one in each zone of the store, for which each of us was responsible every shift, would have made service faster and easier for associates and for customers. But we didn't have enough. Since our complaints about lighting and ladders were falling on deaf ears, what was the point of asking for more of these as well?

Maybe they were just too expensive? There had to be a logical reason we didn't have more of them, so I looked online and found a supplier.

Each cost $4.75.

* * *

How did my coworkers feel about all this?

Retail, certainly at our low level, doesn't really lend itself to introspection or philosophizing. What is there to say? You like it—enough—to stay and do what they tell you. Then, when you can't take one more minute and, hopefully, have found another job, one that pays a lot more, you quit.

We all knew that every conceivable aspect of the store's operations and contents was decided by people we'd never meet, way above our pay grade. This also undermined Joe's authority, as no matter what we asked of him, or how much he might hope to keep some of us, the company granted him considerably less power than we'd thought or expected.

The constant cheaping-out on even low-cost, low-tech tools and the persistent lack of interest in our feedback also contradicted every professional tenet I'd learned or felt. Hadn't we been hired to do a great job? If not, why were we here? I always wanted to know a lot more than, clearly, we would ever be told. I read the business sections of *The Wall Street Journal*, *The New York Times*, and the *New York Post* every day, eager to know how retail, as an industry, was faring throughout the recession. I read *Forbes*, *Fortune*, *BusinessWeek*, *Inc.*, *SmartMoney*, and, occasionally, *The Economist*. I listened to *Marketplace*, a business show produced by American Public Media. I always wanted to know so much more about what we were doing and why and when.

But, on the rare occasions when I'd try to talk with my coworkers about the company, or about how retail was doing in the larger economy, they smiled indulgently and returned to more pressing matters—like that night's pro basketball, football, or baseball game.

It's said that the measure of employee engagement is whether, when you mention your employer, you say "them" or "we." I'd always been a "we" person, but was now working with people who didn't care much, if at all, about how our store, or our company, was doing. There was, from the day I started to the day I quit, no compelling sense that we were really an important part of something larger or *worth* getting excited about. Our paltry wages made clear we were disposable. The company's headquarters were far away in a distant state. We saw district or regional managers only three or four times a year, when we were suddenly hustled into a frenzy of activity to clean the store even more than usual before they arrived. Their hearty, boosterish cheer left no impression on us. The

North Face clearly paid them well and had assigned to them distinct roles within the company. These men (and why were there no women at that level?) had plenty of reasons to care about the merchandise, the stores, the brand, and its success.

Not us.

As a result of this disconnect, their uninterest in our perspective from the floor where we actually sold their products, we became, or remained, disengaged. Their visits felt like troop inspections, a general seated in a jeep whizzing past us, all of us snapping to attention while—to them— we remained a vague, obedient background blur.

We were mere infantry, our jobs to run into the bayonets when the generals told us to.

I soon learned this dismissiveness was normal in retail.

Even the best-known, and often much-admired, retail chains can treat their employees' health and safety with a chilling nonchalance. In a J.Crew store, I overheard a conversation I couldn't quite believe. I introduced myself and asked the associate to repeat what he had just said— that a female customer, furious that the store had run out of gift boxes on Christmas Eve (the night of full-on last-minute shopping insanity), threw a full, heavy shoe box across the counter at the manager.

"Of course you called the cops, right?" I asked. "That's assault."

"Oh, no," he said. "That's not store policy."

(When I asked Mel Kleiman, a consultant who specializes in hiring and retaining associates, about this, he essentially shrugged. "If a customer is already that agitated, confronting them is only going to escalate things," he said.)

Even Apple, typically a media darling, came under scrutiny in March 2010 when a Manhattan sales associate said that actor Richard Belzer, a star of the TV show *Law & Order: Special Victims Unit*, had grabbed her by the shoulders and choked her. Milan Agnew, twenty-one, told the *New York Post*, "He lunges in and grabs my neck. It was no gentle manner. There is no gentle manner to grab someone's neck."

Belzer denied and dismissed the story, even though Agnew filed a harassment charge with the New York Police Department.

While the retail workplace leaves workers vulnerable to physical injury, it also harms them outright—sometimes for life.

Joyce Cohen, a Manhattan freelance journalist, started working at a Starbucks in that city as a barista, for the health benefits offered to part-timers as well as for a regular income, in November 2000. She loved the job and the company. But three years later, the store where she worked removed its carpeting and draperies—and the sound-absorbent properties they added to that space, for workers and customers alike. In 2006, they installed noisy ovens right behind the cash-register area, and in 2007 added loud ventilation and new wall tiles that further amplified the sound, according to a lawsuit Cohen filed against the company in 2007 in New York.

The ambient noise of her workplace so damaged her hearing—*permanently*—that she was diagnosed with hyperacusis, an extreme sensitivity to even normal levels of sound. Her dream job, and employer, had become a nightmare. Cohen liked her job, and she needed the income and affordable health insurance the company offered. She asked Starbucks to accommodate her condition by lowering the music volume, adding gel mats to absorb sound, letting her work farther away from the ovens, and by allowing her to wear sound-muffling protection over her ears.

They fired her. But she won her suit, successfully alleging that Starbucks had discriminated against a worker with a disability—one caused by her place of work. Her hearing was forever damaged by a company she specifically chose for its generous health benefits.

Many retail workers also face the emotional wear and tear of daily dramas from their coworkers, bosses, and customers.

In April 2010, seven baristas, nearly the entire nonunionized staff, walked off the job from Gorilla Coffee, a popular spot in trendy, upscale Park Slope, Brooklyn. Their absence forced a sixteen-day shutdown. The workers quit over what they called a "perpetually malicious, hostile and demeaning work environment" under Carol McLaughlin, one of the store's owners. The other owner, Darleen Scherer, admitted her partner's style could resemble that of "a drill sergeant." The store reopened, but only after the attendant media coverage offered a rare glimpse into the darker side of the register, one usually invisible to happy customers.

There are a depressing number of ways retail workers—*America's third-largest workforce*—are mistreated, invisibly, inaudibly, and indelibly.

Like stiffing them out of their paychecks.

Low-wage workers are "routinely denied proper overtime pay and often paid less than the minimum wage," reported *The New York Times* in September 2009. A survey of 4,387 low-wage workers in New York, Chicago, and Los Angeles conducted in 2008, financed by three foundations, found the typical worker had lost $51 the previous week through wage violations, out of average weekly earnings of a meager $339—a 15 percent loss in pay. Workers earned a median wage of $8.02, more than three-quarters of them making less than $10 an hour—and $10 an hour is itself poverty-level wages.

Women were found to suffer this indignity far more frequently, with African-American workers cheated of their wages at a rate *nearly three times that of whites.*

Of the eleven offending categories of low-wage employment, retail stores and drugstores came in third, with 26 percent of workers reporting this underpayment

One of the ironies of "protecting shareholder interests"—the mantra with which every publicly traded major retailer staunchly defends its rock-bottom wages—is that the U.S. economy still relies so heavily on consumer spending. If you don't pay your own workers enough to meet their basic monthly bills, they're not going to buy jeans, TVs, and other material goods. Workers without disposable income can't afford to shop.

It is shortsighted and elitist to assume that no retail worker has ever invested, or considered doing so once their circumstances improve, in a retail company's stock, whether through individual equities or a mutual fund.

Associates and their extended families are also current or potential shareholders. Their opinions, and their money, should also matter.

Thundered a *Times* editorial, "The report paints an acute picture of powerlessness." The editorial noted the considerable economic effects. "When their paychecks are systematically bled by greedy employers, an entire community's vitality is sapped as well."

Theft from retailers—euphemistically known as "shrink"—was reported to be spiking in December 2009 at $36 billion a year as employee crime and shoplifting made newspaper headlines and the recession refused to end. The study's author, criminology professor Richard Hollinger, told *The New York Times*, "We have met the enemy and he is us." But retailers' own predatory practices, such as paying poorly for hard work while churning through workers, were also feeding into this spike. Hollinger told the *Times* that overall theft is greatest among retailers with high turnover rates, many part-time workers, and younger workers—all of whom may feel little or no loyalty to their employers.

The *Times* story quoted a national study of 106 retail chains' response to a questionnaire: employees were responsible for 43 percent of store losses, shoplifters for 36 percent.

By May 2010, *RetailWire*, an online industry newsletter, reported that criminal activity at retail was still growing as retailers cut back their loss-prevention (LP) staff by as much as 50 percent. Thieves knew very well their chances improved with fewer store staff keeping a skilled and wary eye on them. One expert, Gus Downing, told *RetailWire*, "The real problem has been the actual reduction of sales staff in the store. We literally have tens of thousands of stores in the U.S. opening each day with only one staff member on duty. Here lies the real opportunity for thieves, and I assure you this is where they go."

I felt the sting of this trend firsthand when I read my December 2008 annual review, a formal six-page printed document rating my skills in twenty areas, including two focused specifically on preventing theft. On a scale of one through five—with a two meaning I needed to improve—I got dinged for not paying close enough attention to shoppers' possibly larcenous behavior. I was furious. We had been severely short-staffed during the holidays of 2008, so busy we didn't stop running from the start of our shift to its end. I refused to sign the review and had a long conversation with Joe. Why should I take the hit for not working security when there were so few of us on the floor we could barely serve the customers who *weren't* stealing? (He agreed to change my rating.)

Retailers routinely forbid workers who see a thief in action from doing anything more than alerting a manager, a "no chase" policy that protects the retailers from liability but makes a mockery of their insistence that workers keep an eye out for shoplifters. Without on-site security guards authorized and physically able to give chase, what's the point?

As the recession began to hurt sales, retailers from Starbucks to a national bookstore chain also decided in 2009 to revive a time-honored—if worker-loathed—practice known as Taylorism. It is a style of work named after the American industrial engineer Frederick Winslow Taylor, whose 1911 book *Principles of Scientific Management* established fundamental methods for managing assembly-line factory work. Now, reported *SmartMoney*, "cashiers are rated on scans per minute, while stock workers are timed for shelving efficiency . . . The rules dictate how fast employees work, what they say, even how they move."

The point of super-efficient workers? You can use even less of them, and for fewer hours.

(I now much better appreciated the truth of a sign posted at my local car wash, one where workers scramble in and out of vehicles to vacuum and clean them: WARNING: DUE TO A SHORTAGE OF ROBOTS, WE USE HUMAN BEINGS. THEY CAN BEHAVE UNPREDICTABLY WHEN ABUSED.)

The difference in pay between low-wage workers and those above them creates its own challenges, management guru Stephen Covey told *RetailWire*, "The very question needs to be sincerely discussed in small groups throughout the organization so that we don't end up with such compensation extremes. Mutual benefit, or the idea of win/win, is foundational to trust and sincere, non pseudo-democratic approaches."

Some companies that pride themselves publicly on excellent customer service do so on the backs—and paychecks—of their own employees. Nadira Husain, a forty-six-year-old suburban mother of two in New Jersey, worked for a national chain of department stores renowned for their impeccable commitment to customer satisfaction, one which famously includes accepting returned merchandise anytime in any condition.

Husain, who earned 7 percent commission and who sold $2,500 to $6,000 worth of women's clothing per shift, was pulling in daily wages of $140 to $420—that is, until customers returned the merchandise after they'd (often) clearly worn it, costing her directly, as those hard-earned commissions were culled from her paychecks. Her return rate was 17 to 23 percent, severely reducing the amount she could earn, no matter how attentive or conscientious her service. She loved her coworkers, but hated a corporate policy that punished her while encouraging and rewarding shoppers' bad behavior.

"You don't realize how deeply it will affect you until you're on the sales floor. I'd say thirty percent of my customers abused the policy. I was shocked by it. I was never abusive as a customer. They behaved like shysters! They were the prettiest women, friendly, well turned out, but they all did it," she says indignantly.

Working for this respected retailer, she says bitterly, "was a colossal waste of time. All people quit for the same reason—management whoring down to the customers to keep their numbers up."

Like Hassan Jarane, owner of the gourmet food store Mint, Husain is persuaded the mall environment itself feeds into a greedy, selfish mindset. Shoppers just see one more faceless megacorporation that won't feel a thing if they abuse generous return policies—not the sales associate whose warmth, charm, knowledge, and skills made that sale happen, and whose paycheck takes the hit.

Says Husain with a sigh, "There's no warmth, pride, camaraderie, or relationship-building."

She now works for a small neighborhood clothing boutique, which she gratefully describes as "good fun," and doesn't miss the mall at all. "If our store was in a mall it would lose its essence," she says. "People now want something personal. They're sick of malls. When they go shopping, they want an outing."

Lively, funny, frank, high-energy, smart, and great-looking, Husain's a perfect saleswoman. "Personality matters! You increase the chance of a customer coming back to you if you show genuine friendliness, not sales pressure. I think that's monumental now. There has to be an element of human touch these days when you part with your money."

With thirty years' sales experience, Husain thinks retail managers must shift their priorities. "If people want bricks-and-mortar [in-store shopping] to survive the Internet, they have to reevaluate the associate and the store manager. Treat them with respect! Pay them better! You have to reevaluate your model and not just base it on numbers."

Setting impossible sales goals is another efficient way to ensure worker frustration and drive persistently high turnover. When customers stay away in droves, as they began to in the fall of 2008 with the recession starting to bite more deeply and dampen consumer confidence, how are even the best-trained or most eager workers able to sell *anything*? One J. Crew associate working in a Northeast store told me her daily sales goal was never lower than $3,500, regardless of the season, the weather, sales, or promotions. "They push us constantly and they never say thank you," she said with a sigh.

Jacqueline Alvarino's first retail experience, working for LensCrafters for three months before being fired, was rough. "It's a confidence-killer!" She found it impossible to meet their sales goals, which ranged from $2,200 to $3,000 a day. "They were so high! Didn't they know it was a bad economy?"

She knew LensCrafters' name and products, and felt confident she was making a good bet after passing two job interviews "with flying colors."

Like many associates, Alvarino was handed daily and weekly sales goals, with no explanation. A bright woman, she describes herself as "non-confrontational" and "very reserved," so she never pushed for answers as to why they were often so high, and so unattainable. She quickly grew to hate the company's oppressive management style: "It reminded me of my studies of Communist China." In public meetings of twenty staffers at all levels, employees were required to participate in "self-criticism," then write their deficiencies on a poster for everyone to see. "It seemed humiliating."

No matter how hard she tried, Alvarino—a top student at a demanding university—was deemed unsatisfactory. "Every day they complained about something. I was told I didn't have proper critical thinking skills, that I was inarticulate, that I just didn't understand things, that I wasn't working enough." (This is a young woman offered a full ride to complete her doctorate at Vanderbilt.)

"It was a really strange work environment. I never expected it from a big company like that. I ended up feeling anxious every day."

EIGHT
THIS JOB CAN KILL YOU

If there were a patron saint of retail, it might be Jdimytai Damour, a thirty-four-year-old sales associate from Queens, New York, who was killed November 28, 2008, at a Walmart in Valley Stream, Long Island, after a stampede of Black Friday shoppers shoved him to the ground, leaving him unable to breathe. Other workers were trampled as they tried to rescue him, but angry customers stepped over them, furious that the store was closed because of his death, police and witnesses said. At least four other people, including a woman eight months pregnant, were taken to area hospitals for observation or minor injuries.

Police said about two thousand people were gathered outside the store at five a.m. as Damour opened the door and was trampled to death for his trouble.

One witness, Kimberly Cribbs, told *USA Today* that shoppers were acting like "savages." She reported that when shoppers were told that they had to leave because an employee had been killed, "people were yelling 'I've been on line since yesterday morning.' They kept shopping."

Damour, who stood six-foot-five and weighed 270 pounds, probably looked like a good choice for crowd control. He didn't stand a chance. He had been in the job for a week.

In December 2008, his family filed a lawsuit against Walmart, alleging that store ads offering deep discounts "created an atmosphere of competition and anxiety" that led to "crowd craze." The suit claimed that the company "engaged in specific marketing and advertising techniques to specifically attract a large crowd and create an environment of frenzy and mayhem."

Amid the flood of comments, 669 in all, on the *USA Today* report of his death, one solution suggested opening the store twenty-four hours to prevent congestion. Shoppers, it seems, are insatiable.

* * *

Working as a frontline retail associate places workers in job-specific danger, says a researcher for the National Institute for Occupational Safety and Health. There are four ways retail workers typically lose their lives on the job: they are killed by a burglar or shoplifter who enters the store, someone unknown to them; they are killed by a coworker; they are killed by someone using the facility where they are working (that is, a customer); or the intimate partner involved in a domestic dispute, most often a male, comes to the workplace to wreak vengeance.

Two-thirds of retail homicides are committed in the course of a robbery, and convenience stores, where workers are alone late at night, are often a target. "They experience a lot of crime," the researcher told me in an interview. "Employees are not trained how to protect themselves, and there are programs and strategies to do so." These include training in cash-handling, improved lighting, visibility, access control, the work environment, and signage. Many retailers do know a variety of effective measures that might make their workplaces much safer, but they don't act on them.

The push for better worker safety, I was told, usually doesn't come from the retailers relying on these frontline employees. "There's a real push now for researchers to work with organizations and unions, now that we know programs can prevent crime. We work with community groups like the Chamber of Commerce or the Korean Grocers' Association," the researcher said.

It's too bad, then, that so few retail workers—most of them in grocery stores—*are* unionized.

The Occupational Safety and Health Administration (OSHA) offers weekly fatality reports; in only one month, three retail-related deaths appeared: on December 28, 2009, when a worker was shot by an armed robber in Jamaica Plain, Massachusetts; on January 16, 2010, when a store attendant at Speedy Petroleum in Indianapolis was fatally shot during a robbery; and on January 28, 2010, when at 2:47 a.m. a worker in Max Convenience Stores in Louisville, Kentucky, was also shot during a robbery attempt.

According to the Bureau of Labor Statistics' Industry Injury and Illness Report for 2008, the incidence rate of nonfatal occupational injuries and illnesses in retail is highest at building material and garden equipment and supplies dealers, with a 5.8 percent.

Working in an elegant and upscale store in a wealthy, low-crime neighborhood offers no protection. In 2007, Sandra Pumarejo, fifty-two, a wife and mother working as a bookkeeper at Michael Dawkins Jewelry on East Sixty-fifth Street in Manhattan, was stabbed there eighteen times. Her killer was David Andrango, an illegal immigrant who ran errands for the store and whom she had caught stealing $10,000 in raw gold—offering to let him repay it over time if she did not call the police to report his crime, he told police after his arrest.

In January 2010, a robber burst into another Upper East Side jewelry store and fatally shot a seventy-one-year-old worker who refused to hand over any gems. Henry Menahem was shot in the chest and was pronounced dead a half hour after the shooting. The thief grabbed items worth $1 million and fled. The theft occurred in a part of Manhattan

The New York Times called "the land of the doorman, the dog walker, the nanny." The shop was about three blocks from the town house of New York mayor Michael Bloomberg.

The store, R. S. Durant, had no security camera.

In December 2007, nine people were killed and four severely injured when a gunman rampaged through the upscale Von Maur Department Store in Omaha, Nebraska. The shooter, who killed himself, was seventeen-year-old Robert A. Hawkins; his attack was the state's deadliest since 1958. Two employees were critically injured. Mickey Oldham, sixty-five, was shot in the back and stomach but returned to work in the store. She was fired in April 2010 because she could no longer stand for long periods of time.

"Mickey has been and will continue to be compensated through a variety of sources," the privately owned store said in a statement. "Although Mickey is no longer an employee, Von Maur deeply appreciates and values her past services and commitment and cares considerably about her well-being."

* * *

Ask retail veterans—analysts, authors, consultants—to name the best retail employers, and Costco always makes the very short list. I called them to find out why at 3:47 on a Friday afternoon, the start of the 2010 Memorial Day weekend.

Within fifteen minutes, a lively, funny, down-to-earth guy—whose name I didn't catch but whom I assumed must be the poor flack who didn't get to start his weekend early—called me back. It's well known that Costco pays its associates some of the highest wages in retail, and I asked him how such numbers were achievable.

"Our lowest starting wage is eleven dollars an hour and our average is nineteen sixty-five an hour," he told me. The decision to pay hourly workers well had been made decades earlier when the company was founded, he told me. "Even back in the sixties, we decided that if you provide a living wage and decently priced health benefits you'll find good people and you'll keep them." The average wage for retail and grocery store clerks (many of the latter unionized) is $13.50 to $15 an hour, while discounters like Sam's Club and Walmart are far below that. The pressure to cut associates' and cashiers' wages, he said, was indeed tremendous and relentless. "Wall Street constantly asks us, 'Have you tried eighteen an hour? Or seventeen-fifty?' We're not going to do it because it's not the right thing to do. Happy people are our ambassadors on the floor."

Ninety percent of Costco's employees are hourly workers, half full-time and half part-time. Unlike other retailers, who demand split shifts and overnight work and cut hours as often and deeply as they feel is necessary, with little or no warning, Costco guarantees its part-timers twenty-five hours of work per week. Their churn rate—workers quitting—used to be 20 percent (much lower than the rest of the industry) and is now 11 percent, he says.

"It's harder!" he said. When retailers face such pressure to keep raising profits, he admits, "It's harder to do it this way."

The company gets as many as three thousand to six thousand applicants for every new store opening, with perhaps two hundred fifty positions available, he said. "We can't interview all of them, but we might bring in ten times the number of applicants we need for any one job. Half of the fit is only something we can discover by talking to them. That's part of our job!"

His company's personal, democratic approach to low-level hiring is also now almost unheard-of—certainly for so large an employer. Most competitors of Costco's size rely only on computers and psychological tests to weed out most of those seeking a job. "That's not us! Not everyone has a laptop or knows how to use a computer at the library," he said.

Who was this candid, friendly caller?

Richard A. Galanti, the firm's chief financial officer. A man running a company with $73 million in sales, with 137,000 employees in 600 locations, had called me back? Quickly? Directly? (A call to Kip Tindell, CEO of The Container Store, another retail employer much admired for how it trains and pays associates, was returned by a company PR rep who made it clear I was hopelessly naïve to ask for ten minutes of his time—he needed six months' notice, she said, to find that much for me.)

Costco is able to pay its workers so well because they cut corners elsewhere, operating no-frills stores with cement floors and by not advertising. Most retailers spend 2 percent of their sales revenue on ads, while Costco passes those savings on to consumers.

When Home Depot CFO Carol Tome gave an interview to *Fortune* in August 2009, she made it clear that treating their associates well was a priority: "We wanted to make sure that we kept our associates, the men and women on the floor of the store, totally engaged. In an environment where a lot of companies were cutting back, we said no. We are going to invest in those associates. We're going to pay merit increases, pay bonuses, make contributions into the 401(k) plan. We're going to be singularly focused on them so they can take care of our customers . . . Investing in [them] was a decision . . . Reducing our support staff was a hard decision. We lost 10 percent of our officers."

Her choice was highly unusual—protecting and nurturing associates? She continued, "What is the point of difference inside the store? It is really that belly-to-belly experience between the associates and the customer."

Can a retailer offer shoppers value—and still have values?

In-store labor represents only 8 to 13.5 percent of retailers' costs, according one software developer who works with many of these firms.

Yet, while retailers spent $270 billion in 2008 on advertising and promotion, many associates continued to collect pennies. Eric C. Wiseman, the CEO of VF Corporation, the parent company of The North Face, Vans, Jansport, and other well-known brands, collected a total compensation package in 2009—according to a report in *The New York*

Times—of $6,412,327. Other retail CEOs did nicely: Steven A. Burd of Safeway made a total of $9,383,003; Kevin Mansell, CEO of Kohls, took home $9,037,962; while Howard R. Levine, CEO of Family Dollar Stores, claimed $5,612,726.

When our hours were cut back to the minimum possible allowed under The North Face's rules—five hours a week for part-timers, leaving us gasping for air as the recession worsened and few others were hiring—its parent company, the VF Corporation, reported *The Wall Street Journal*, sat on $382 million in cash.

Retail is an industry filled with consultants, vendors, analysts, commercial Realtors, and others pulling down healthy incomes, some of them while turning a blind eye to its hypocrisies and pay inequities. One software firm's CEO—who works with many of these retail giants—explained, "The store buyers get treated with kid gloves. The merchants [who travel overseas to source and buy products for their retail employers] are treated like princes. They are a small set of people spending millions of dollars, so they have lots of power. Why can't they pay [associates] more? They'd rather spend their budgets on their buyers. A lot of credibility is given to buyers, more than is rightfully theirs. I think more money *should* be given to the selling side, but as long as the culture is like this, it's not going to change.

"There's a huge cultural barrier there. They [the buyers] make a fortune whereas the poor sod standing for eight hours in the store is making no money. This is the challenge we have—we pay you like crap, we make you stand there all day, customers treat you like crap. Nobody cares about the associate! It's highly improbable that retail will treat people as human beings."

Sadly, what he says is true. It took me a long time to understand this—who really wants to acknowledge how unappreciated they are by the companies raking in huge profits, and run by CEOs making millions, who need their skills and labor as much as that of their C-suite executives? But when low-level workers like associates are paid so little for their work, that work is de facto worth less to their employers. Why bother making sure their workplaces are clean, safe, well lit? Why bother protecting them from verbally, even physically abusive customers? They'll only quit soon enough. Someone's always desperate for a job.

It's a quick conceptual leap from worth less to worthless.

NINE
COGS IN THE MACHINE

Working in retail means resolving and accepting—or ignoring—a welter of contradictions. Senior executives earn multimillion-dollar compensation packages, while those who make and sell their products earn pennies, by comparison, per hour, week, or month. Associates earning $7 or $8 or $10 an hour, no commission, sell $700 or $1,000 worth of items to the wealthy. Whatever we buy, we're all complicit in someone's employment—and potential exploitation.

Every shift, as I unpacked clothing manufactured and shipped from across the globe—Peru, Malaysia, Jordan, Mexico, China—I tried to picture the people who had packed it in the same plastic I was about to throw away. The last set of hands, perhaps, to touch the same garments I was unfolding in a suburban New York mall were those of a worker earning in a week or even a month what I made in an hour or a seven-hour shift. I often wondered about these invisible, distant workers at the opposite end, the first links in our company's global supply chain. They relied equally on our cheap labor.

What were *their* lives like?

American journalist Kelsey Timmerman visited the clothing factories, and workers, who made some of his own clothing and shoes in Honduras, Bangladesh, Cambodia, and China. The result is his 2008 book *Where Am I Wearing?*, a sobering reminder that what associates in North America consider dull, poorly paid work pales in comparison to the conditions and pay of those making the products we sell on the floor.

Timmerman found that the average Cambodian garment worker earns $60 a month; one man was supporting his family of seven on such wages. The Cambodians he met making Levi's jeans were earning $12 a week, and in China he found workers making shoes earning $140 to $225 a month for an eighty- to one-hundred-hour week.

They remain distant strangers, people we can't picture, easily rendering their concerns distant and abstract.

At the turn of the twentieth century, writes Timmerman, "the workers fighting for their rights were our countrymen. We shared a flag, a language, a culture . . . Producer lived with consumer. But today, we share little with the people who make our clothes . . . divided by oceans, politics, language, culture and a complex web of economic relationships. If they are overworked and underpaid, it doesn't affect our daily lives as it [once] did."

Out of sight, out of mind.

Until, in a rare moment of supply-chain transparency, word of the brutal working conditions for Chinese workers at Shenzhen firm Foxconn, making some of the best-loved, best-selling technology brands like Apple, Sony, Dell, Nintendo, and Nokia, made international headlines in late May 2010. Eleven workers there had committed suicide; their giant Longhua factory, the world's largest, had three hundred thousand workers assembling goods.

"We are not a sweatshop," said Terry Gou, fifty-nine, who founded Foxconn in 1974. "A manufacturing team of 800,000 people is very difficult to manage." Gou told the London *Daily Telegraph* he planned to hire two thousand therapists to counsel his workers.

Instead, in June, the company moved much of its production to

Langfang, in northern China, while starting construction on an entirely new company compound a thousand miles inland. There, they knew, labor is even more plentiful, cheaper, and less demanding. The company left behind in Shenzhen what Reuters called an "industrial fortress," complete with banks, bakeries, post offices, restaurants, shops, parks, and dormitories catering to more than a quarter million workers.

The official Xinhua news agency reported that the new Foxconn plant under construction would produce mainly Apple iPhones, generate more than $13 billion in annual exports, and have a production capacity of two hundred thousand handsets a day. Wei Wei, deputy director at Personnel Exchange Center, a major job recruitment center in Zhengzhou, said Foxconn had asked his firm to help recruit one hundred thousand workers within three months' time in preparation for the first phase of the giant factory's expected opening in 2011.

Ever-cheaper foreign labor is a moving target for any shoppers who care to consider the origins of their clothing and the conditions under which it was made. China's wages are not the world's lowest, competing for that dubious title with Bangladesh, India, Cambodia, and Vietnam.

After the Foxconn suicides, it looked—briefly—like the balance of power might actually shift in workers' favor as the company hastily promised raises and better working conditions. Emboldened, other Chinese workers elsewhere even went on strike, winning unprecedented wage and other concessions from their employers.

By June 2010, though, the multinationals were flexing their muscles once more and promising to shift production to the cheapest possible countries, reported *The Wall Street Journal*: "Rising labor costs in China are forcing U.S. apparel and accessories retailers such as Ann Taylor Stores Corp. and Coach Inc. to consider relocating at least some of their production to countries with cheaper work forces." Guess, Inc., also told the *Journal* it was considering building production capabilities in Vietnam, Cambodia, and Indonesia.

Accommodating Chinese workers, the *Journal* reported, might boost apparel retailers' costs 2 to 5 percent a year. "It's a really bad time for labor costs to be rising," Jeremy Rubman, a retail strategist with consulting firm Kurt Salmon Associates, told the *Journal*. "Nobody wants to alienate the consumer that's finally coming back."

Yet a few retailers are choosing to make candor about their labor practices part of their appeal to consumers, like JF & Son, a small clothing store in Manhattan, owned by three twentysomethings who have everything made for them in a studio in India. "People want to know how the things they buy are produced," Jesse Finkelstein, one of the owners, told *The New York Times*. "I think we have a responsibility to our consumers to offer this level of transparency."

In *Where Am I wearing?*, author Kelsey Timmerman singles out Mountain Equipment Co-Op, a national Canadian outdoor clothing chain, for devoting significant time, attention, and resources to issues of fair labor practices. The company, a cooperative run by a nine-member national board, has a full-time staffer devoted to ethical sourcing, with an annual budget devoted to this of $200,000. Still, their Web site admits:

> Our persuasion with suppliers is also limited. In 2009, we bought $65 million worth of product from 80 contract facilities. For a handful of factories, we're a big customer, and our bark has bite. But for the rest of our supply chain we're tiny, and our requests are prioritized relative to other, larger buyers.
>
> Improving working conditions is a multi-faceted and time consuming process. It involves everything from changing how a factory operates to the way managers and workers think . . . The individuals who make these products and the ones who benefit from them are largely strangers to one another. Nonetheless, what binds us together is not really the bike that is made in Taiwan and ridden in Montreal or the tent that is pieced

together in Ho Chi Minh City and later erected in the Canadian Arctic. Rather, it's the common aspiration for something better, both for us and our fellow human beings.

How many shoppers even care about the distant, invisible workers who create most of the products we buy? Are any of us willing to pay for our principles?

Labor economics professor Robert Pollin has calculated that increasing apparel workers' pay in Mexico by 25 or even 30 percent, writes Ellen Ruppel Shell, "would raise the price of a shirt in the United States by 1.2 percent . . . a leap in price of a $20 shirt to $20.24 . . . But few multinationals have been willing to put it to the test."

The gap between American workers and their domestic employers is also widening, writes *New York Times* labor reporter Steven Greenhouse in his 2008 study of American employment, *The Big Squeeze*: "Industrialists were once firmly in control . . . but now investment bankers, mutual fund managers, hedge fund managers, and increasingly, managers of private-equity funds wield great power and are forever pressuring the companies that they've invested in to maximize profits and take whatever steps are necessary to keep stock prices at their highest. Companies, in response, often skimp on wages, lay off workers and close operations."

Nikki Baird, a retail analyst with RSR Research in Boulder, Colorado, studied how 160 retailers, of all sizes and types of product, were managing their workforces, for a report she produced in 2007. She wrote, "Retailers talk the talk—they have high aspirations for the role that employees play in their customer service, *the number one opportunity identified by survey respondents* [italics mine] . . . The workforce ends up being treated as a means to an end, rather than a strategic asset."

I shouldn't have been shocked by Baird's report, but her candor—as someone who's also worked the register herself—was striking. "Our survey respondents clearly see their workforce as a means to an end—a tool of customer service—and not an end in itself (where happy employees mean happy customers)," she wrote. Asked to list the top three priorities driving their workforce management strategy, 58 percent of retailers included increasing top-line sales and 55 percent listed improving customer service—but only 21 percent mentioned reducing staff turnover. Yet 59 percent said they have trouble finding good employees and 50 percent struggle to keep them.

"Retailers' . . . goals are not turning into action," Baird concluded. "Retailers have no way—and seemingly no desire—to identify the brightest of the bunch [of employees] and tempt them into a retail career. [They] leave a lot of opportunities on the table."

Part of the challenge is making retail attractive as a career. When *RetailWire* asked, in March 2010, why this is so difficult, retail veteran Doron Levy, president of Captus Business Consulting, replied, "It's up to the store's leadership to create a functioning retail workspace. And you can't spell functioning without fun. Retail is 90 percent a morale game, and if you don't have it, you aren't running on all cylinders. Good workers will flock to companies that provide fun and functioning work environments."

When Darienne Page, who at twenty-nine has one of the world's coolest jobs as the West Wing's receptionist, wants to evade job-related questions, she tells them she works at Walgreens, a drugstore chain.

"No one asks, 'Oh, what do you do at Walgreens?'"

"It's not looked at as a career per se," agrees Deborah Weinswig, a retail analyst for fourteen years with Citigroup. This despite managerial salaries, even at Walmart, that can hit $150,000 plus bonuses, she says. Weinswig follows nineteen major retailers, and finds customer service, even at the high end, so lackluster that more and more shoppers are buying online.

The single greatest problem in retaining staff, according to RSR's Nikki Baird? Constant staff churn doesn't appear as a line-item cost. When retail executives can't quantify the cost of replacing 40 to 100 percent of their staff every single year on their balance sheets, it doesn't enter their business calculations. Only costs—such as labor—receive careful attention, with a relentless focus to reduce or eliminate them entirely.

It's a practical as well as conceptual problem, creating industry-wide turnover at a level even analyst Weinswig finds "a bit shocking, very high." Churn, and the untrained, unmotivated workforce it nurtures, remains a rogue elephant stampeding through retail's living room.

Working as a retail associate—certainly for any major company—means being reminded daily that you're merely one tiny cog in an enormous global machine, from the workers six time zones away stitching apparel to the equally invisible, distant CEO collecting millions. You're completely disposable. As every industry expert I spoke to reminded me, you're *meant* to leave. The job is designed, like some dysfunctional combustion engine, to consume cheap labor and spit it back out again within weeks or months, the spent fuel of a ceaseless sales cycle. This affects managers as well—when 100 percent of your staff will probably disappear within a year of starting work, what's the point of getting to know them? Why would associates invest much energy trying to climb a career ladder? There *is* no ladder.

That became clearer with every meeting in our store, which was held once a month, at nine a.m. on a Sunday morning. Attendance, for everyone, was mandatory, even for those who had worked all day or night Saturday. Each time we met, several associates wandered in around nine-thirty or so, annoying people like Tam and me who had made it a point to arrive on time, only to wait around for the others. Some arrived clearly and unapologetically hungover, reminding us what a range of coworkers Joe had to manage. They'd get "written up" for being late, but the threat clearly held no menace.

At the first few meetings, Joe tried to lighten our mood—which I appreciated—by bringing in coffee and doughnuts. But that soon stopped. And the tone of the meetings was overwhelmingly grim and negative.

The managers stood in a row opposite us, creating, deliberately or not, an unusually formal "us versus them" vibe. It felt like their one chance, en masse, to remind us all, suddenly and jarringly, of their positions of authority. It was uncomfortable and disorienting, as we usually all got along easily, bantering and teasing one another regardless of rank or title.

In the meetings, things were different.

Joe, usually easygoing and upbeat, now played the heavy: "Too many people are calling out. They're doing it at the last minute and leaving us to fill their shift. That's your responsibility.

"The store is a mess. It's your job to make sure it's absolutely spotless before you leave at night. I keep finding clothes on the floor."

There was nowhere to sit, so some of us would lean or perch on the credenza, many staring at the ceiling or their fingernails or, the boldest among us, smiling or rolling our eyes at one another. The meeting was always a one-way conversation, filled with the false urgency of corporate's latest push to sell a particular jacket or pair of pants.

Our opinions or concerns? Largely irrelevant.

"Why can't they just send us an e-mail?" Tam hissed in my ear at one meeting. Indeed. Being dragged from bed on a Sunday morning only to be chastised was hardly a morale-booster.

After Joe rattled off our failings and our newest marching orders, we'd all sign a sheet attesting to the fact that we'd heard them.

Praise was rare. Only when I pushed him—knowing that our store was always in the top three or five in sales of *every store in the chain*—would he grudgingly commend us. I'd look around the cash wrap to see if anyone else cared. I saw little evidence that they did. Mostly, they just wanted to get out and go home, start their Sunday, or restart it, with their husbands or girlfriends or kids. We were paid to attend the meeting, but the amount of time it took most of my coworkers to travel there by public transportation tripled the time commitment—and their resentment of this intrusion on their private time.

Wasn't our clear, consistent excellence something worth noting and celebrating? Didn't it show corporate and our own team how terrific and effective we were? Why didn't Joe ever praise us?

We needed to hear some hard-earned and well-deserved good news, too.

In response, I started speaking up during the meetings. I liked Joe personally, and had enjoyed many long conversations with him whenever we shared a shift. But the meetings were the only place and time when managers could have made us feel like a team, acknowledging publicly how well we were doing, even while making necessary criticisms and corrections.

I didn't like challenging a superior so publicly, but I quickly grew tired of Joe's relentless negativity during the only moments he had his entire team together in one place. You could see the effect it was having on our morale. My speaking up annoyed Joe, and I knew it. But no one else, even when they felt the same, dared say much, grumbling instead beneath their breath like sulky children.

It was clear that Joe's jovial manner depended on us not directly confronting him in these meetings. But mentioning our concerns privately produced no changes. And the meetings offered us the only opportunity—most of us working totally different shifts—to see or even get to know one another, and to compare our individual impressions. Once we were working on the floor or in the stockroom or at the registers, there was little time or privacy in which to do so.

I felt safe speaking up because I worked only one night a week and, more important, consistently sold well; my numbers were high, proving my productivity. I routinely sold $120 to $140 per hour; my best shift was $542 an hour. I was late maybe five times in over two years and "called out" sick perhaps three times. I started to see how unusual this was—partly because I never had to cope, as several of my coworkers did, with relying on multiple modes of public transportation or a sick child or a caregiver who didn't show up.

So, while others examined their shoes or their manicures or giggled to one another during the meeting, I'd ask Joe about missing equipment or the lousy lighting in the stockroom. Most of my coworkers, it seemed, didn't care or didn't want to risk looking difficult.

It really didn't matter much what we asked or wanted. We rarely got answers.

Add to our monthly come-to-Jesus meeting the daily inanity of how the store was run. The stockrooms were forever crowded, disorganized, jammed with garment racks and boxes and loose plastic bags. Someone, somewhere, for no reason anyone ever understood or explained, had decided that a third of the merchandise should hang on racks so high it was just below the ceiling, the garments all facing out shoulder to shoulder along the perimeter of the sales floor like some Middle Eastern bazaar.

None of us could reach the merchandise without a shepherd's hook, and we didn't have enough of those.

Zeke, our friendly merchandiser, who had moved to California, was replaced by Melissa, a chilly blonde so thin her shoulder blades jutted through her cotton T-shirts. New to New York, unable and unwilling to chitchat with us, she made clear we were mere associates, there to do her bidding, folding, stacking, and rehanging every single item when, where, and how she told us to.

Why, exactly, did Melissa tell us to move merchandise from its hangers to stacked piles or vice versa? None of our business. No one dared ask. And so, one especially absurd afternoon, we spent an hour removing a wall filled with slick, slippery nylon men's jackets with two large stripes running the length of each sleeve, a look appealing, perhaps, in Bulgaria circa 1983. Unsurprisingly, our affluent suburban shoppers and their preppy sons had left these monstrosities mostly untouched.

As we took them all down and packed them for shipment to our outlet store, we pulled out their replacements—slick, slippery nylon jackets with stripes on the sleeves.

Every few weeks, a district or regional manager blew into the store, prompting our sudden terror that he would find fault with something. They always did. So did the "secret shoppers," people whose MO was obvious to everyone who had helped one before—they were markedly fussy and demanding and always returned an item within minutes of purchasing it.

The opportunities for praise, encouragement, and financial rewards were few, the odds of punishment for some minor infraction always high. The whole thing felt truly Sisyphean.

In his book *The Big Squeeze*, labor reporter Steven Greenhouse interviewed several low-level retail workers. A few, naïvely and hopefully, had given it their all, and ended up bitter, broke, and broken. "Corporate executives, intent on maximizing profits, often assign rock-bottom labor budgets to the managers who run their stores and restaurants, and those managers in turn often squeeze their workers relentlessly," he writes.

Greenhouse profiled Drew, a former military policeman who worked for Walmart in southern California, for a gas station, and for Toys "R" Us.

"It seemed like a nice, relaxed retail environment, and the mall was very nice," he said. Drew enjoyed Toys "R" Us, but later went to work for Family Dollar, which has more than sixty-three hundred stores nationwide. He was hired to work as a store manager, but quickly realized that the software program used by corporate to delegate labor, Matrix, had decided two people were sufficient for his needs to unload four thousand items an hour from delivery trucks, about twenty-two seconds per box. He went to work for Rentway, a store offering goods on monthly installment plans. He was fired for lending a customer $3 to make her payment.

"I'm so disappointed with the retail world—they've broken every covenant with the American worker," Drew told Greenhouse. "I long for the days when you worked for a company and the company was loyal to you and you were loyal to the company."

TEN
WHOSE IDEA WAS THIS?

I t can take a week, a month, a year, or a decade. When working in retail starts to pall, it's tough to turn back the clock and regain whatever initial enthusiasm you brought to your work as an associate. Maybe you were convinced your hard work, energy, high sales, and product knowledge were sure to help you climb the ladder, promotions and raises a logical next step. But they never came. Your coworkers, the people you liked and laughed with, quickly disappeared, either being fired or deciding to quit, sapping morale as your team shifted and changed. Constantly adapting to new personalities and styles loses its charm. Your managers, saddled with new additional responsibilities by their corporate head office, were increasingly busy, distant, and distracted. They spent almost all their time in the office, answering faxes and e-mails and staring at a computer screen. No one had time to coach or mentor you, even if they had the skills or interest.

You didn't realize it's a mug's game. *You're not expected to stay.* A whole new fresh crop can and will be hired, each as eager to impress employers and shoppers as you once were. Why bother to keep weary veterans?

I was initially impressed with my job at The North Face. We received four days' paid training, capped by a good meal and a chance to social-ize with one another. We were trained every quarter, ensuring we knew new products and could answer most of our customers' questions. We were given free clothes and shoes to wear. Our managers were generally friendly, warm, and down-to-earth. We had good products to sell.

Then prices on some of our pieces jumped significantly. Savvy shop-pers, the brand-loyal folks who knew the names of our clothing styles and proudly bought new pieces every year, asked us why; they knew what these items cost. We had no acceptable answers. "The company wants more profits?"

As the recession deepened and many shoppers snapped shut their wallets, we had to work harder than ever—with fewer, more reluctant clients—to persuade them of the value of already high-priced nylon and fleece made for pennies per hour far overseas. The recession was hitting hard, but the ways in which we were expected to sell did not. The river of new products forever flooded our stockrooms without any acknowledg-ment from the powers-that-be that we were now often pitching a wary, nervous customer. People, now, would eat up an hour of our time—and walk out empty-handed. Several told me their purchase would have to wait until their next paycheck. Many more were now paying in cash.

After Zeke left and Melissa took over his job, even the store's mer-chandising suffered. Zeke was fun, cool, and friendly, while Melissa thought she was really special. For hanging, stacking, or folding a bunch of clothes in ways that someone in corporate told her to? Undressing and re-dressing fiberglass mannequins didn't require a PhD. The skills involved were *what*, exactly? To us, she was just one more boss snapping out orders, another one we saw rarely, didn't know, and didn't like. Nor did she care. No one wants to take orders from someone half their age with poor social skills and an inflated ego—at rock-bottom wages, there's no upside.

And who had decided that a third of our clothing should hang so high that none of us could reach it? What logic of design or sales savvy dictated this? Had it never occurred to anyone anywhere in this enormous, multinational, forty-year-old company that this made shopping slow, annoying, and boring for consumers? That it made selling the clothes difficult and cumbersome? That every time we reached up for a jacket just beneath the highest shelves—the ones covered with thick layers of dust—that same dust would float down and stick to the garment we were trying to sell? We could barely reach the apparel. Cleaning the highest shelves themselves? Impossible.

The total disconnect between what associates value—whether better pay, promotions, benefits, or a more inclusive management style— and the ruthlessly profit-making goals of most parent companies soon becomes insurmountable. I heard this from every clerk I interviewed. *No one wants to feel worthless*, but the thin veneer of corporate welcome, if there even is one, wears off fast. In an economy that has pushed millions of formerly middle-class professionals into long-term unemployment, foreclosure, and despair—with banks cutting off lines of credit and slamming those who still have one with brutal new user fees—pushing a company's (highly profitable) 28 percent APR store credit card has become an act of fiscal violence.

Nor do weary, worried, newly frugal shoppers want to be bullied or cajoled into their previously spendthrift ways.

After a Banana Republic clerk on Newbury Street, Boston's upscale retail strip, asked me twice in five minutes in April 2010 to open one of these absurdly overpriced store accounts, I snapped impatiently at her, fed up with this greed. Cautious consumers are smarter now; rote phrases that worked effectively for the free-spending, credit-reliant, pre-recession consumer now insult both shoppers and those who serve them.

Times have changed. But many retailers, desperate for profits, are sticking to old scripts.

As every single consultant told me, many of retail's senior executives still consider their faceless armies of associates disposable. Since the work is hard, dull, repetitive, and poorly paid, anyone who takes on that job—the unspoken logic seems to suggest—should know better *and leave.* Soon.

And what I, a journalist who had written on business for *The New York Times*, was reading daily in the business press—how retailers were now bending over backward to offer consumers fantastic service—frequently was at odds with my own experiences. In the Saks in Greenwich, Connecticut, credit card in hand, ready to pay $200 (a fortune for me) for a Diane von Furstenberg silk blouse, I tried in vain to actually get a sales associate to sell it to me and walked out annoyed, disappointed, and empty-handed. In Pottery Barn Kids, shopping for my mother during the holidays of 2009, I had to climb over boxes and negotiate an obstacle course to reach the cash register, where a snarky associate asked me pointedly, "Is that all you're buying?" At Anthropologie, instead of a gracious smile and a thank-you for my business, the associate snarled, "Is that *it?*"

Excuse me?

In our store, several of my favorite colleagues had left within the first year. Only one, Mariel, had been professional enough to give two weeks' formal notice. Everyone else simply stopped showing up, even if they were on the schedule. No one called or e-mailed or even simply said, "I quit." This passive aggression was immature and depressing. Was this what working for The North Face had driven them to? Or was this just the caliber of colleague I'd be stuck with if I stayed?

I thought of applying to other stores where I might earn commission and make a lot more money; concerned friends, knowing how high my sales were, urged me to do so many times. But I know myself well enough. I wouldn't last a week faced with the princesses I'd have to placate. Our area's wealthy, demanding shoppers simply wouldn't get any nicer, no matter how much larger my paycheck. Nothing could mitigate their toxicity.

My dignity was costing me a fortune.

An associate older than me working in a local fabric store told me of a young woman who snapped her fingers at her, demanded to be shown "that fabric I liked last week," and, when asked if she might be a little more specific (she could not), complained to the store manager that the associate—a calm, helpful veteran—had been rude to her.

I had seen firsthand how retail can quickly extinguish an associate's sense of joy, pleasure, and anticipation. I used to bounce into the store every Tuesday afternoon eager to see who I was scheduled with, hear how their week was going, see what mix of shoppers we'd get that day. I was curious about our new merchandise and how it was selling.

After a year or so, I realized that I faced a choice, one I didn't want to make. I could—as many of my coworkers did, and had many years earlier—simply shut down emotionally. Not really care about the work, the products, the brand, or our customers. Offer a fake smile, ask rote questions, and barely listen to the answers. Connecting sincerely took too much time and energy. And, when customers suddenly turned vicious, you felt stupid for being human and genuine, leaving yourself vulnerable.

If I was to stay in retail, maybe moving to a better-paid job elsewhere, I'd have to steel my soul as I had to for years in journalism. *But I longed to connect.* Only in those moments of connection was the dull, mechanical, unchallenging rest of it—folding, sleeving, sweeping, sensoring, sorting, stacking—worthwhile.

This irresolvable conflict between the best of the job and the worst of it was ruining retail for me. I was starting to fray at the edges.

One day I railed at Jorge for making a mess of his section. He looked at me placidly, with some real, friendly concern for my eroding mental health. "It's just not that important," he said. "You can't care this much."

He was right.

You might love the products, store, coworkers, managers, company, or any one of these. But when so many customers are toxic, and management allows their abuse to continue unaddressed, retailers lose even the most ambitious or committed of employees.

That's, ultimately, how they lost me.

ELEVEN
CUSTOMERS FROM HELL

There's no way past it. Working as a retail associate, whether in a chic Madison Avenue boutique filled with $5,000 dresses or at a Walmart in rural Iowa, is like joining the infantry. You're cannon fodder. Whatever private, unplanned drama some customer feels like casting you in that day—you're stupid/you're rude/you're slow/you're incompetent/she hates the product/he hates the store/it's Tuesday/it's rainy/it's sunny/she has her period—you're it. You didn't audition for the role of psychic punching bag, and you really don't want the part.

Too late.

The question is, how will you handle it? If it's your own store and you're managing a small staff, it's your call. One shop owner in a wealthy Connecticut town told me he'd twice had to call the cops, so obstreperous had some spoiled customers become. But at a chain store in a mall? You're a cog in the machinery and everyone knows—and takes advantage—of it. The minute something goes south, like you run out of gift boxes, customers get ugly and make the ultimate threat: to call company headquarters to complain about you. No one wants the boss to get in trouble, and it's your boss who's running that store. So you fake-apologize, day after day after day after day, just to shut them up. Some walk into the store pre-pissed, annoyed by the weirdest things, things you have no knowledge of, no control over, and no way to communicate to senior management.

Like:

"Your jackets are too short!

"You had it last year!"

"Don't you have another purple?"

"I wish this had pockets."

Customers expect you to listen attentively, caring deeply that your heartless and mismanaged (yet somehow highly profitable) company has thwarted their most arcane personal desires.

And, at wages so low that an hour of your labor won't even buy you a consolatory movie ticket or a few beers, your primary task often feels like it's not about selling products or services but mustering the stamina to suck up—or, more likely, shrug off—whatever craziness customers throw at you, a façade of professionalism and politeness your daily armor.

I'd never been so tested. I'd worked some of the toughest and most competitive stories in journalism—in torrential rain, in ninety-degree heat and humidity, in the Arctic in minus-thirty cold. I'd researched and written twenty-five hundred words in a day on issues so complicated I needed scientists to backstop me. Worked in French, on crutches.

But this job was starting to bruise my soul in ways I could never have imagined—because I could simply not have imagined how nasty one stranger could be to another.

I'm not a frail flower. Few who know me would describe me as weak; quite the opposite—I've been told since my twenties that I appear intimi-dating, brimming with unshakable confidence. I spent most of my child-hood, ages eight to thirteen, at boarding school and summer camp, in each instance surrounded day and night by relative strangers, some of them desperately miserable and determined to make anyone unfortunate enough to cross their path equally unhappy through whatever means possible: bullying, taunting, shaming, gossip, or innuendo.

Then I arrived at my Toronto high school halfway through tenth grade, joining a conservative group of kids who'd been attending the same schools from kindergarten. They had no idea what to make of me. And boys! They were an alien species to me after so many years of single-sex life. I was verbally bullied for three years by a gang of boys who couldn't figure out why I, a shy, pimply newcomer who wore funny clothes (six years in uniform can leave you a little fashion-challenged), bristled with academic confidence nonetheless and refused to kowtow to them because of their gender.

Determined to put me in my place, like sick little Winston Churchills, they never, ever, ever gave in. Every day brought a fresh volley of the same tired insults, which they shouted at me down the echoing hallways and hissed at me in class. The teachers knew, and did nothing to address or to stop it. To these bullies, I was a "dog," my new name "Doglin," a dog biscuit even laid atop my desk. By the time I graduated, with the delicious triumph of a cool boyfriend, good friends, and the sweet irony of being named queen of our senior prom, my soul was nonetheless deeply bruised.

I'd survived all that, and more. How tough, then, could the public be? But working retail showed me, to my own embarrassment, that those years of unanswered insults had left a deep, simmering pool of rage within me.

I knew retail work would certainly expose me, like everyone working with the public, to unpleasant or rude customers. I expected that. We've all had bad days: a crappy diagnosis, a flunked exam, overwhelming debt, a lost job, chronic pain—there's a million reasons someone might be bitchy to a stranger for no obvious reason. As someone who's suffered months on end of chronic pain from orthopedic surgery and recovery, which seriously drained my energy and my patience, I understand.

But what I didn't anticipate was random vitriol. I'd rarely, if ever, encountered such bare-knuckled verbal hostility. If I did, as a private citizen, I shouted back, called for help, or quickly fled. (There's no fleeing in retail. Where are you going to go? Home?) And Canada, where I grew up and lived to the age of thirty in Toronto and Montreal, two large, diverse cities where I worked as a daily newspaper reporter, was then a safe and fairly friendly place. Fewer people there, certainly in cities, own or carry guns than in the United States. The entire country only has thirty-four million people competing for jobs and resources, not ten times as many. There's also a wider, stronger, and deeper social safety net, and everyone, everywhere, has cradle-to-grave government-supplied health insurance. People just aren't as verbally aggressive as Americans, let alone sharp-elbowed New Yorkers. They don't have to be, and we Canadians, wherever we live, find such behavior ugly and unnecessary.

Toronto had a pretty low crime rate when I lived there, so I didn't spend my life cringingly anticipating violence. I didn't even stop to consider when or how such work-related aggression would happen. And so every time it did—call me naïve and unprepared—it set me back on my heels. Like the middle-aged Caucasian man who came into the store and pointed to a jacket on a mannequin, high atop a shelf.

"I want to buy that," he said.

"I'm sorry, we can't sell the clothing on the mannequins," I said.

"Can't? Or *don't want to?*" he said with a sneer. "I thought you were here to sell things." His tone was so nasty he felt dangerous. I walked away and found Angela, our assistant manager. I stood discreetly distant from him and turned my back, making sure he couldn't overhear me or see my facial expression.

"Nutcase, behind me," I warned her.

I wasn't accustomed to having someone else fight my battles for me. But neither was I in the mood to become someone's psychic sponge. Let the managers handle it.

Every time someone bit our heads off, we'd have to shrug and move on. How much could we ever really relate to customers, any one of whom might be carrying emotional nitroglycerin? We would start out with a friendly greeting, yet within minutes they might be threatening to call corporate. It was exhausting, and increasingly so over the years, dealing with such unpredictability. No wonder we all started to shut down emotionally, faking our friendliness and saving genuine feeling for our private moments. *You had to.*

One December day in 2008 brought me as close as I'd ever come to quitting. It also brought me to tears. I didn't cry when the *Daily News* fired me. I cry at funerals. I cry with anxiety when they wheel me into orthopedic surgery. If I cry more than a few times a year, that's a lot.

The day began with an annoyed woman in her sixties, elegant, wearing a fur-lined vest and a thick strand of amber beads. As required to prove that each of us was meeting our individual daily sales goal, I asked her, "Did anyone help you today?"

It's a fairly straightforward question.

"No!" she shouted. "And I wish someone had!"

I rang up her purchase, wrapped it, handed it to her. I could have stopped there, and maybe should have.

How lousy could her day have been already? It was barely eleven a.m.

"Can I ask you a question?" I said, kindly, calmly.

She looked stunned and grateful I even cared to probe further into her discontent.

"What happened?"

"An associate walked away from me when I asked for help," she said softly.

"Wow. I'm sorry. That's completely wrong. No wonder you're upset."

She left, mollified.

The rest of the day went well, busy with holiday shoppers, but nothing we couldn't handle. I was working from eleven a.m. to eight p.m., a shift I liked, as it gave me enough time to run some errands before work. Nor did it require sticking around for the slow agony of closing, which could add forty-five more minutes to the end of the day. By that point, we were sweaty, fed up, fried, and ready to go home.

That same night, a guy came to the counter, gray-haired, well dressed, with his son, a young man of perhaps eighteen or twenty.

"Did anyone help you today?"

"No. I guess that means we get a discount, huh?" His tone was sneering, provocative. *What was his problem?*

Did he really think his line original? Or even amusing? We'd heard it all before. And, in his triple-ply cashmere, this guy needed no break from us. I didn't like his bullying demeanor.

"So, you work on commission, right? That's how you make your money?"

He seemed determined to keep needling me. Like a fool, I took the bait. I was alone at the counter and there was no one to hand him off to and walk away, my preferred MO.

"No, we don't get commission."

"Wow. So, what do you get?"

"We have daily sales goals we're expected to meet," I explained.

"What happens if you don't meet them?" he persisted. "If you don't get commission, I guess the real prize is—you get to keep your job!" the man crowed.

They left the store and I stood there, weary to my bone marrow of being one more stranger's punching bag.

I turned to Carl and Bill, desperate for a kind word.

"Well, you're going to see something you've never seen before. No one's ever seen it at my workplaces. I'm going to cry."

I *really* needed a shred of understanding or empathy. They didn't say a thing.

It was 7:40, twenty minutes to the end of my shift. I had already met my sales goal by five p.m., and had exceeded it, as I often did, and as usual, no one even noticed. I went into the shoe stockroom, found a beige metal folding chair, sat down on its cold bare seat in that dingy, dark, silent space—and wept. I cried for twenty minutes, sobbing alone into the darkness.

I was done. My right shoulder, on which I'd had surgery the previous May, still ached all the time, even after months of healing and physical therapy. I was sick of being treated like garbage, like an illiterate moron, like someone with no options or skills or accomplishments or worth. I was sick of having to hurdle, every single shift, day after day after day, people's insulting assumption that we were all nothing more than human trash.

I was tired of never fighting back, biting my tongue bloody with the retorts they knew we couldn't say. Even in high school, the bullies sure to find me every day, I at least had pals to comfort me who knew I was much more than "Doglin." The bullies here weren't teen boys but adults, driving $80,000 cars and sending their kids to fancy prep schools to make sure they would never end up in my position, in my sweaty, dirty, ugly, worn-out, company-supplied sneakers, my feet throbbing with pain after five or six or seven hours running, running, running all day long.

If any of these people had ever worn a plastic name badge or worked in a low-wage service job, they'd long since repressed that lousy, depressing memory.

It felt sometimes like they enjoyed punishing us for even being there, an irony when 90 percent of shoppers still make their purchases—whether a gallon of gas or a pair of Louboutin pumps—face-to-face with others; even today, only 10 percent of shopping is done online. We must be stupid, lazy, unmotivated, have lousy educations and no ambition. Why else would anyone ever take so thankless a job? Why did they feel compelled to remind us we were bottom-of-the-barrel?

I speak fluent French and Spanish well enough that I used to translate and interpret for Chilean refugees seeking asylum in Canada after they'd been tortured. I'd traveled to thirty-seven countries, written a well-respected book about women and guns, and I'd won five fellowships. Carl had taken care of a severely disabled sibling, Joe had served in some of the most terrifying military operations imaginable, and Tam had worked three jobs while pregnant to earn her living. None of us deserved this casual contempt.

I'm really not a crystals-and-rainbows kind of girl, posting little affirmations on the mirror each morning Oprah-style: I *am* a good person! I have worth! I *am* lovable!

But I was starting to see the appeal. With so many customers so determined to make you feel like shit, it took a soul of steel to shrug it all off.

My colleagues were just as fed up with this as I was, our shared, private motto of solidarity: "I am *not* your personal slave!" Like them, I was sick of being underestimated and overlooked. Of people leaning over the screen of the computer every single time I entered their e-mail address, certain I couldn't possibly spell it correctly. I was tired of people telling me how to spell the names of their wealthy towns like Chappaqua (home to the Clintons), as though they were wildly exotic and unfamiliar locales in deepest Turkmenistan I couldn't possibly ever have heard of—instead of a town where I'd eaten lunch a dozen times at the same French bistro the Clintons enjoy. The restaurant had even hung my photos of Paris on its walls for months. I'd watched Bill Clinton one night enjoy a rapt audience of customers—his Secret Service guys barely feet away from him, and me—in its vestibule.

So, that night in the shoe stockroom, surrounded by twenty-foot-high stacks of boxes of boots and sneakers, I wasn't really crying over one stupid man and his vicious tongue. Nor because my feelings were especially hurt that evening; I've heard so many cruel and caustic things in my life that his jibes weren't new or original. I also knew his animus wasn't personal—that people like him are like sharks, forever cruising their world for something wounded and bleeding, something easy to attack.

I was just worn out.

And, of course, this being retail, there was much, much more of this yet to come. The worst part, for me, was how utterly random and unpredictable it was. You'd have a friendly, lively conversation with a customer you totally enjoyed. You were both feeling great, loving the whole thing—and, *wham!*, the next customer could be pissy as hell before you even said, "Hi!" This roller coaster was bizarre, as though you'd been strolling down the street with a good friend on a sunny afternoon, relaxed, when someone, without any warning, grabbed you from behind, holding a knife to your throat.

Why are customers are so unbelievably nasty to those working in retail?

Because they can be. There are remarkably few public places in which a functioning adult can, as they say in psychology, decompensate. Throw a hissy fit. *With impunity.* Little children do it all the time, throwing tantrums at the drop of a hat. They're little, they're tired, they don't know any better. But a grown-up—a tax-paying, home-owning, two-hour-a-day-commuting professional—lives a tightly controlled life with no room for error. Your husband/wife/partner/kids/dog/cat *need* you to step up to the grindstone every single day. Your mortgage is $7,000 or $9,000 or $12,000 a month, plus another $30,000 a year in taxes. Plus $25,000 per kid for private school. Your family really doesn't want to watch your neck veins bulge with rage. It scares them. So what better place to let loose those pent-up demons?

The mall, baby.

The customer is king/queen. Whoever said, "The customer is always right," was wrong. Customers are often rude, aggressive, lying, pushy, whiny, demanding, and insulting. They've lost the receipt or gift card or coupon or are trying to return a ten-year-old garment or one their daughter just wore to the prom.

Most people shop alone. Their bad behavior, like the kid who shatters Mommy's best vase and hides the shards, remains safely invisible to the people whose respect they need. In space, no one can hear you scream. In retail, everyone has to.

We can't retaliate. In the nation premised on the audacity of hope, whose fundamental creed of social and economic mobility remains deeply cherished, where anyone with hard work and persistence can rise to the top, retail associates are a visible reminder of the bottom of the food chain. Until you've unshackled your ankle from retail, you're easy pickings for anyone whose day, or life, isn't going terribly well. They know you need that shitty job.

We can't spit in your soup. Think about it. Eat out anywhere and be an asshole. Invisible mayhem *will* be inflicted on your meal before your waiter brings it (back) to you. You rarely see the same level of naked aggression in a restaurant, whether in a diner or at Daniel, as you do in a store. What are we going to do? Stab you with a sensor tag pin?

People are miserable. In their jobs, their marriages (or singlehood or mid-divorce or premarital jitters). They have a bully boss. Or they just got fired. Or they're about to get fired. Or their spouse is having an affair. Or they are, and just got caught. Life in the United States in the worst economic downturn since the Depression, when millions still can't even find a job, when fresh graduates carry six figures of educational debt, when people are terrified of losing their home or car or line of credit, is no picnic. So some are desperate to off-load their anxiety and rage. You can't scream at the Fed for lowering interest rates so low you can't live on what's left of your retirement savings. You can't shriek at American Express for doubling your APR or at the bank for refusing to expand, or even give you, a line of credit. *Someone* has to suffer—voilà, the associate!

* * *

Here's the challenge that retail posed for me. I really love engaging people in authentic conversation. It's what helps make me a good journalist: people tell me the most extraordinary things about themselves because I make them feel safe in so doing. It's been like this since I started writing professionally at the age of nineteen, when one of my first assignments for a national women's magazine was to find and interview women who'd faced terrible tragedies, like their husband dropping dead in front of them or having their house burn down. I learned young to find a way to make total strangers comfortable with me within minutes.

While selling, which is the essential skill of all good associates, I listened carefully. I actually *did* care about what people said to me. Not *everything* all the time—some people are really boring—but so many are so starved for a little kind, undivided attention they positively blossom if you actually give it to them. So, when I offer my genuine attention and interest, it's a decision and it's a choice. It's also damn rare in almost any store I've ever visited.

I also expected basic respect. Even though I was working in a shitty job at lousy wages doing basic work, I expected civility and recognition of the fact that I was at least working, and working hard, whether on behalf of shoppers or The North Face's management. Like all my coworkers, I also shopped in my private time for shoes and clothes and food and liquor and gas. We'd all received crappy service. We worked hard, as our company expected, to give a lot better than we usually got. We knew how bad it was out there.

Serving non-Americans was always the worst. Those born, raised, and educated, as I was, in more professionally hierarchical and less socially mobile nations—where if you're at the bottom of the barrel professionally the odds are high that's where you'll stay for life—shopped in our store according to their cultural norms. In their worlds, where postsecondary education is free or heavily government-subsidized, where fewer people have to take and cling to a horrible job they hate, maybe one far below their skills, just to get health insurance, we *must* be the lowest of the low.

In other words, they treated us like crap.

In the United States, it's entirely possible to rise from a crummy, low-paid job to CEO. People do, and we all know it. Which, at its democratic, Horatio Alger best, can foster a healthy sense of respect for even the lowest-paid among us who actually show up clean, sweet-smelling, and sober, regularly and on time, and do a good job and do it with a smile.

Not so for many of the Europeans, Middle Easterners, Latin Americans, and Asians I served. Maybe my coworkers had a totally different experience, but many of these customers made sure to remind me of my station and how much lower it was than theirs. They would barely look me in the eye, whether on the sales floor or when handing over their credit card, ever so carefully, as though my lowly status might rub off on them.

A Spanish woman came in, wearing a thick, lush, glossy full-length fur, shouting into her cell phone with a perfect Castilian accent, her *s*'s becoming "eth's." Our store, even at the best of times, was crowded and so, deciding she simply needed more personal space, she impatiently shoved a huge, heavy, loaded display rack filled with garments away from herself.

Into me.

I made it a point to treat everyone equally, whether they were wearing worn-out jeans, filthy sneakers, and a tattered cotton hoodie or spit-shined Guccis and a $500 Burberry casual jacket. Our customers, a feature of the job that I always really enjoyed, were an extraordinarily wide mix of ages, races, and income levels: Boy Scouts, high school, college, and grad students, teachers, physicians, attorneys, cops, psychologists, sports professionals, tourists, visiting businessmen from Sweden and Finland and Iceland and Switzerland and Britain and France. I loved this variety. It was like playing a familiar card game, with some elements comfortingly predictable, others less so. Every week reshuffled the deck—back-to-school, holidays, vacation shopping—and offered us customers with a slightly different set of needs and requests. We also got plenty of working-class and blue-collar folks, men and women with thick calluses and grimy fingernails, working on ships or trucks or construction sites. They, too, needed warm, sturdy, waterproof clothing that would last a few seasons. I enjoyed them all equally.

Wealth doesn't impress me. I grew up with it, around it, at school and at camp. My family had it. My ex-husband made a very good living, even as a young doctor. We shopped at Saks, vacationed in France. I attend a church with people whose incomes dwarf mine—one parishioner wrote a personal check for $250,000 to buy us a new organ. Whatever. In my own world, manners, kindness, talent, hard work, humor, humility, generosity, and creativity are what truly impress me. You can have bags of money and no real values.

And, growing up in Toronto, where old money and serious wealth is likely to show up in battered corduroy trousers or a Shetland crewneck sweater—as it still does some in Yankee enclaves—had also taught me to never judge people only by their appearance. Too many of suburban New York's well dressed, in their Michael Kors and Prada and Gucci and Tod's and Cartier, were also people up to their eyeballs in credit card debt, one paycheck or two away from declaring bankruptcy, no matter how costly their jewels or clothing. And how breathtaking their arrogance. I also knew that money doesn't buy good manners, often quite the reverse. Some of the kindest and gentlest customers I'd met lived far, far away from Greenwich or Scarsdale.

But one older couple, an Asian man and his wife in their late fifties or early sixties, was weird from the start. They came into the store looking at jackets. I waited the requisite few minutes before approaching them to ask if they might need any help. Because we didn't get commission, and because I almost always not only met my sales goals but doubled or tripled them, making any one particular sale was never a big deal for me. I wasn't in a rush and I didn't sell hard; not my style, nor the store's.

They ignored my question posed directly to them, as though I simply did not exist, even though I stood a few feet away. I returned every ten minutes or so, so they wouldn't feel ignored—standard procedure. But these two, who kept talking to one another in their own language as though I were both invisible and irrelevant, radiated entitlement. Had they secretly arrived in sedan chairs?

The man thrust a jacket he didn't like at me, not even looking at me, as though I were his personal valet. They stayed in the store for forty-five minutes, obsessing over the same garment, trying it on and taking it off again. One of our many responsibilities was foiling shoplifters, which required a delicate balance between leaving people undisturbed and sticking close enough to prevent theft. By the third time I went back to check on them, the woman snarled at me, "Don't rush us!"

The name on their credit card as I processed their sale was that of their local nail salon.

What this instructive encounter really did was make me appreciate the respect and kindness with which my own boss here, Joe, treated me from the start. I couldn't imagine him treating any employee so demeaningly and had never seen him do so, even in anger. It was obvious this couple, business owners, took for granted docile, terrified workers.

These put-downs also came with a racial flavor. I saw it every single shift with my coworkers, all of whom—except for three part-time white college students who worked at the store only briefly—were black or Hispanic. We all wore name tags. It was part of our uniform and our names were to be fully visible at all times. For whatever reason, customers rarely bothered to *read* the tag or use the associate's name when I asked, ringing up the sale, which person had helped them.

"The tall guy. The thin girl with the short hair. The guy in the plaid shirt."

No one ever dared say they'd been helped by a young black woman, a Hispanic man. They'd mumble or point vaguely or shrug off the question. We were invisible and anonymous. But not when they sought someone in authority. Customers of all ages simply assumed I was the manager because I was white, older, and female. Every time, I'd defer to Tameisha or Bill or Jorge, the full-timers who knew the products and where to find them—which changed almost weekly—better than I did. When a nonwhite store employee answered them, even if my colleague was standing right beside me, customers ignored him or her and kept on talking to me instead. It was racist. It was rude. It was dismissive of coworkers with more years' experience and much deeper product knowledge. But my white face was some sort of reassuring beacon. I'd know what I was talking about!

My coworkers hated this pattern, but we could do nothing to change it.

By my third and final holiday season, December 2009, counting the days until I could afford to quit, I almost came to blows with a customer. More than two years of their insults and sneers had worn away my initial goodwill and patience; I'd become a rotted-out bridge ready to collapse under the weight of just one more vehicle.

It was November 30, 2009. She was morbidly obese, dripping sweat, a white woman, fiftyish, with stringy, uncombed gray hair. She approached the cash wrap with a pair of shoes.

"You need to get a shoehorn," she whined. "I couldn't get the shoes on easily."

As I'd learned to do by then, I didn't respond, as there's really not much to say. Customers complain so often about so many things you really can't listen thoughtfully to all of it, even most of it, let alone respond. Your head would explode.

I asked her, as required, for her zip code.

"I live across the street from the mall!" she snapped.

There's only one residential building opposite the mall—a psychiatric hospital. That seemed about right.

I didn't know the zip code for this town because I didn't live there. I just worked there, part-time. I'd memorized, from repetition, the zip codes for Greenwich—06830, 06831, 06832, 06836—and Scarsdale—10543—because I'd heard them so many times. We had relatively fewer customers from the town where the mall was located, or I might have known it. But I didn't.

"I don't know that zip code," I said calmly and pleasantly. "May I have your zip code, please?"

"Don't you pay income taxes? Don't you file tax forms? You work here!" she shouted.

"I'm simply asking you because it's part of my job to do so," I said, my voice still calm. *You cow.*

"You're making me really upset!" she shouted.

"Funny thing, so are you," I finally said. I was done.

"You're being hostile!" she hollered.

"*Hostile?* You have *no idea* what my idea of hostile looks like!" I exploded, fleeing to the farthest corner of the store. I was embarrassed, ashamed of my loss of control, furious at myself for allowing her to provoke me. And furious that no manager had stepped in to defuse the situation and soothe her.

Fire me. Really. Just fucking fire me.

I headed to the stockroom, shaking with anger, humiliation, and disgust. I didn't care what happened next. I wasn't going back out there for a while. Poor Tameisha was in the break area eating a chocolate bar and trying to chill out. The last thing she needed was me huffing and puffing with indignation. In a blind fury, I stabbed a pen deep into the side of a cardboard box of fresh holiday stock. Brian came into the stockroom. I was in no mood to explain the debacle to a kid half my age, so new to the store—even as assistant manager—he didn't even know the stock yet.

"Tell me your side of the story," he said placidly. "I've heard hers."

"Is she going to call corporate?" I asked.

"She might. She said she was thinking about it."

Why was I sticking with this stupid job, with deadened coworkers and managers who turned a blind eye to abusive clients?

I left early, at Joe's kindly suggestion, cutting my nine-hour shift short by three hours. Stick around to make an extra $33? No amount was worth it.

TWELVE
THE END OF MY ROPE

By June 2009, I wanted out.

One night, sleeving jackets alone in the rear corner of the store, I chanted quietly to myself, "Time to go, time to go, time to go." I was worn out, bored, and feeling extremely sorry for myself. I pictured myself, however melodramatically, being given a terrible diagnosis like the one my stepmother had received, and dying within days of the sadly accurate eighteen months doctors had given her. My mother has suffered, and survived, several kinds of cancer, so I spent plenty of time wondering when, or if, it might hit me as well. Would I really want the final memories of my life to be those of folding boards and dirty shelves? I was now fifty-two, and retirement was a dream Jose and I still hoped was within reach. But it sure wasn't going to happen if I stuck around here. It was clear I wasn't going to rise within this company, and I had no appetite to find another store and start all over again for the same poor pay.

If I didn't leave soon, I wondered when, if ever, I would. Like some spooked trapeze artist now focused on the net and not the next leap, I'd started to cling to my little paycheck and my plastic badge and a warm, safe place to show up every Tuesday, not the writing, editing, and marketing skills that had earned me plenty of income in the past. I was rapidly losing my nerve and my confidence in myself. I needed to reclaim those qualities or risk losing them for good.

One evening mid-July of 2009 I walked up to the cash wrap to find a lean, fifty-something blonde with short hair and bright blue eyes looking at me keenly. She wore a light blue striped muslin shirt, and had a hippie-ish cool unlike most of the women we saw. I knew I knew her from somewhere, but couldn't remember where.

"Hey!" she said.

"Hey, how are you?" I replied cheerfully, trying like hell to figure out who she was.

"You don't remember me, do you?"

"No, I do. But where did we meet?"

It was Sally, the wife of a lawyer I knew socially.

The day was slow, so we could chat. What she told me was sobering, and reminded me why I was still holding on to this job, no matter how tedious it had become. Like me, she had worked years before as a magazine editor in Manhattan, making good money before staying home as a mom. To earn some cash, she'd recently gone out to work for the Census Bureau, making an enviable $18 an hour.

"You can't believe who showed up to work," she told me. "CEOs, really senior guys, people our age with tons of experience. People are really desperate for any work they can find these days."

This blast of cold air from the current labor market—even for veterans with impressive résumés and decades of experience—quickly ended my pity party. I was sick of this job and could do it in my sleep. But at least it was secure, known, and *mine*. And every week brought more bad news as the economy, in recession since the previous fall, tanked even further. By late July 2009, the U.S. economy had cut 6.5 million jobs and the number of involuntary part-time workers (people like me who would have preferred a well-paid full-time job) had doubled to nine million. I read the stories every day in the business pages of *The New York Times* and *The Wall Street Journal*. But it's one thing to read about it, another to live it.

Retail alone had chopped 850,000 jobs since 2008. It made me feel like a Titanic survivor floating amid the wreckage; however uncomfortable I might be, at least I had *something* to cling to.

I also faced my own financial demons, debt, and fear, in addition to watching the journalism industry shrinking. A few months earlier, I had finally settled an out-of-state lawsuit against a start-up publication that had ordered $20,000 worth of work from me a year earlier, then abruptly canceled it as they slid into bankruptcy, leaving me scrambling wildly to replace that income, without success. Then they reneged on $5,600 worth of invoiced stories. I'd hired a collections attorney and finally recouped a percentage of my fees. That left me carrying a credit card balance of more than $6,000 on my American Express card (more than $2,000 of it uncollected pay), now charging an APR of 12 percent variable, soon to rise to 15 percent variable, after decades at 9.9 percent fixed. I'd written another story for *The New York Times* and was eagerly awaiting its publication, only after which I'd get paid—a story about how small business people all over the country were struggling to pay *their* bills as their own invoices went ignored as well. I'd done a lot of freelance work for the *Times*, and assignments from a local weekly section had become a quick, easy, and reliable source of income. No longer. They'd cut the section entirely, and with it I immediately lost one-third of my annual earnings.

Every corner of my own personal economy—future journalism income, debt, the need to keep saving—was looking grim. It wasn't smart to walk away from *any* job.

In the prior year, forty-eight thousand journalists nationwide lost their jobs, twenty-four thousand of them working in print. Many of those were also living in or near New York City, as I did, and were now competing with me for many fewer freelance gigs and job opportunities. Magazines, some long established and well loved, some newer, but all of them sources of income for hundreds of staffers and freelancers, were shutting down almost weekly: *Portfolio, Gourmet, Country Home, Cottage Living, Domino, Fortune Small Business.* Even the bible of the newspaper industry itself, the 108-year-old trade magazine *Editor & Publisher,* bit the dust.

And I didn't want to leave this job on bad terms, in a huff of frustration over yet another lousy customer. I'd worked too hard and too long for that. I liked Joe and I liked my coworkers. I wanted to leave on an up note, no matter how small the paycheck or unexciting the work. Who knew when or if I might need a reference, or even a chance to come back and pull in some ready cash again? My last job, at the *Daily News,* had ended so horribly. *I* wanted to make the choice this time.

As we headed into fall, life within the store was changing in several key ways. Angela, now heavily pregnant, was due to give birth the day before Black Friday—the biggest single day of every retailer's year. She couldn't have picked a worse time. Of course, she hadn't picked it at all. The baby, a boy, had come as a surprise, although a welcome one. And Peter's wife was due to give birth within a few weeks of Angela. He'd be staying, but Angie would be gone for at least three months. In our busiest season, Joe now had to find and hire someone new to take over her spot as "keyholder," someone with the responsibility to open and close the premises.

He needed an assistant manager to take over Angie's job until—and if—she returned from maternity leave. She was making about $45,000, so I figured a few months of netting a steady $2,000 or more per month at her salary level, even temporarily, would have been great. I told Joe I'd like to be considered for the spot: I'd been there more than two years; knew all the staff; knew the products and the company and the store; had demonstrated my value through consistently high sales. He assured me he'd keep me in the mix. When Phil came by that fall, I told him as well. Typically jovial, he assured me they'd think about it.

Of course, they never did. I didn't push, I admit, but didn't think I needed to. They knew me well. But as the weeks went by and no one asked me about it, nor began the lengthy security clearance process necessary for this promotion to happen, it was obvious I wasn't even being considered.

Instead, Brian appeared, a twenty-six-year-old college student with a nimbus of curly light blond hair, pale skin, and light blue eyes who had worked elsewhere as an assistant manager. He was the new Angie. I'd never been in the running at all.

I said nothing to Joe or Phil about this, but the way they'd handled it—by ignoring my sincere and serious request for a temporary promotion—really annoyed me. It felt like a repeat of what had happened to Mariel, a hardworking female colleague who'd also been passed over for promotion to assistant manager—and for which she had considerable prior experience elsewhere—in favor of a younger guy brought in from outside the company, someone Joe knew from another store in the same industry. Two ambitious women, two experienced women with good track records within our company passed over for a reasonably expected promotion, without some discussion about why we were not being considered or what skills we needed to acquire to win one. That was two too many for me.

It was done so quietly and smoothly. Joe didn't like drama, one of the reasons I liked working with him. But I also knew, from several coworkers and from my own observation, he didn't like confrontation. Angie was docile, not one to pick a fight with him, no matter how great her frustration (and it got pretty high, she told me). Everyone, especially Joe, knew I had no such hesitation. I'd confronted him, even politely, at our monthly staff meetings, when almost no one else ever dared speak up. The lighting in the stockroom was poor. We were given insufficient physical tools—like the shepherd's hooks we needed to reach goods displayed high above our heads. If we were always in the top three- or five-selling outlets among the chain's thirty stores, as we had been since the store opened and even as the economy tanked, why were we never praised?

If Joe wanted someone to roll over and play dead, which his behavior made clear that he did, I wasn't it.

* * *

I took a week off in August to visit my father in Toronto. We had a lot of fence-mending to do after his wife's death two years earlier.

I took the train north from New York, a twelve-hour journey, and spent a week at my dad's apartment, sleeping in a narrow single bed in the room that once housed all my stepmother's designer clothes, rows and rows of them lined up on rolling garment racks. I used what was once her bathroom, the cupboards, previously crammed with costly cosmetics, now empty. The place felt a little ghostly, her presence forever visible in the enormous oil portraits of her, painted by my father, staring down from the walls. My dad was a talented artist, and his paintings and drawings, etchings and engravings and silverwork lined every room. A huge canvas stood on his easel, an oil painting he'd been working on for many months. It took pride of place in the middle of his studio, where I couldn't possibly ignore it. But it was almost unbearable to look at.

"What do you think?" he asked.

I could think of nothing to say: it was as bald a statement of his feelings as a scream—a winged, naked man falling to the earth, his wings singed, an Icarus of utter despair.

My father and his wife had enjoyed a long, healthy, blessed life together until the very end. They had lived on a boat in the Mediterranean for several years, then later owned a two-hundred-year-old mansion in the Irish countryside, bought for cash. They had traveled the world, eaten well, drunk fine wines, worn lovely clothes. He had won major awards for his films and television work, both from the Canadian government and from his industry. She, too, was a player in that tight, competitive world, thriving on her status and power. Even in his late seventies, he'd never stayed overnight in the hospital, nor required major surgery, nor needed any medications to maintain his tremendous energy and health. They had a wide circle of loving, loyal friends.

Calamity seemed to avoid them. Her cancer, and her swift and brutal death, were probably, at first, as unimaginable to both of them as a hurricane sweeping through their downtown Toronto living room. Now my Dad was alone, and eighty, trying to make sense of it all in the way he knew best, through making art.

We had a good week. We loved our decades-old rituals: strong dark coffee in the thermos every morning, CBC radio blasting through the kitchen, dinner in the little backyard garden at night, the King streetcar rattling past. We took long, slow walks with Cully, the dog that was Dad's seventieth birthday gift from his wife, along Lake Ontario, marveling at the cormorants and egrets and herons. We even went to the Canadian National Exhibition, a 131-year-old Toronto summer tradition, Canada's largest fair, filled with goats and butter sculptures and llamas and carnies. I hadn't been to the Ex in years, and it was so corny and mass-market I could never imagine my dad going. But we did. We rode the Ferris wheel, ate barbecue, played rigged midway games for hours, betting again and again, laughing at our silliness for even trying, snapping blurry photos. We both needed to heal, although we'd never dream of using such intimate language. A family of professional communicators—our words and images transmitted for decades to millions of strangers—we were all pretty hopeless at expressing private emotions to one another. We'd fearlessly rattle any public cage for a story, but not the ones surrounding our own hearts.

* * *

An exit from my retail job finally appeared.

I'd begun blogging, for minimal pay, in July 2009 for a new Web site called True/Slant, and by November was earning as much bonus money from that blog as my store income. The blog, I hoped, would lead to other opportunities, maybe even, at some point, another full-time job.

In early December, I took a test for the Census Bureau, which was hiring for jobs that would pay $14 to $21 per hour, with forty-hour weeks possible for up to a few months in the spring of 2010. I'd scored ninety-five out of a hundred, a score the proctor assured me was very good and upped my chances of getting a call from them. I only had a green card, and citizens would have first shot at these jobs. But I had supervisory experience, spoke Spanish, and—which shocked me—was only one of about twenty applicants in my town who even took the test. I figured I might have a decent shot at a job with them, should there be one.

My fiancé, Jose, had been worried for many months that, with a hundred buyouts demanded by Christmas, he could lose his job as a photo editor at *The New York Times* after twenty-six years there. We found out on December 17, 2009, that he was still safe, for a while anyway, and in January 2010 a 5 percent pay cut imposed the previous year on many staff was eliminated, boosting our income. That month, we also refinanced the mortgage on our apartment, adding our consumer debts to that sum, at a much lower interest rate than with any of the eight-plus credit cards and lines of credit driving us to monthly distraction. As soon as we closed on that new document, our slavery to enormous monthly debt service would end as we folded all our consumer debt into one low-interest monthly mortgage payment. That, too, eased much of our worst financial pressure.

Maybe I *could* quit.

I'd changed. I was now the customer-from-hell when I wasn't the nicest shopper in the store; having worked the other side of the cash wrap for so long had taught me what great salespeople are capable of. I so rarely saw it. It didn't matter where I went to spend my money. One afternoon, at Saks in Greenwich, ready to splurge an extraordinary (for me) $200 for a silk designer blouse—my credit card at the ready—I couldn't even get the associate to deign to help me. At the huge J.Crew shop on Madison at Forty-fifth Street, bored clerks pointed vaguely when I asked for a specific item. Where was the solicitous service nervous retailers assured us was the new normal? I had yet to encounter it.

Now, though, I also carefully and consistently thanked anyone doing a service job well, from grocery baggers to gas station attendants. I viscerally appreciated how grim it could be, how little many customers thought of them, and how hard and poorly paid was the work.

Occasionally, so rare it was like sighting a unicorn, I met a star associate who was smart, fun, and helpful, like Marilyn, a fifty-something, redheaded comet flashing through my local Home Depot. The place is airplane-hangar-huge, overwhelming and exhausting, and I always dreaded going there. But she whizzed me up and down the aisles, quickly and efficiently helping me find a random assortment of items. It was clear the woman was a gem—and other shoppers tried to flag her down as I had.

"You're amazing!" I told her, grateful and surprised to find a woman, and a woman her age, bopping around this enormous store with ferocious competence. She grinned, clearly proud of her terrific skills and how much they meant to a weary shopper.

"I love hardware," she said simply.

* * *

The end came quickly for me.

In late November 2009, one female customer had been so weird and so nasty—the one who accused *me* of being hostile—that I almost smacked her. As the French would say, *ras-le-bol*! By now my cup was overflowing. My overreaction to her had shocked me as much as it did my calmer colleagues. It really was time for me to do something else—anything else—for a living.

The last straw, of course, came from corporate.

I'd had plenty of customers toss insults and question my intelligence, but never before had felt the need to walk away for good. Now, finally and without any doubts, I did.

I'd been playing softball and, after five innings, limped off the field mid-November with a stabbing pain in my left foot. One of our teammates, an orthopedic surgeon, guessed it was a stress fracture, which an MRI confirmed. It didn't hurt that much, and with a bootie on it I was able to function, even if I walked like a drunken sailor.

I decided to keep working at the store. It was almost Christmas, the busiest time of the year. I'd put up with severely reduced hours for many long months—a mere five hours a week—and now wanted and needed to recoup financially, scheduled for three shifts a week of 8.5 hours, each with only a thirty-minute break. I wanted the cash and wanted to finish my third holiday season, curious to see how the recession would play out.

By November 2, the mall's Christmas decorations were in place and we were gearing up for the holidays. Joe seemed wearier than usual. We'd had a visit from his boss's boss's boss, a manager so senior we'd never seen him or even known his name until then. It had prompted the usual Potemkin Village frenzy to get the store into a condition we prayed would pass inspection, even though we all knew it never did.

"It's retail. They're always looking for something wrong," Joe said with a sigh. It didn't seem possible that any of us could be working any harder. This was a soldier who had served with the Special Forces. If *he* was worn out, maybe there was a good reason for it.

I asked Joe if I could use a small folding stool, which I could sit on for a few minutes at a time while at the register when my right leg got too tired from supporting all my weight. Unable to exercise as often or as vigorously as usual, I'd gained some weight, which only made things worse. He agreed.

The next week, as I stood behind the register, he told me the stool had to go: Phil, the district manager, felt it was a dangerous impediment behind the counter where someone might trip over it.

"Are you fucking kidding me?"

I rarely used that sort of language with Joe, and certainly nowhere near customers. He was shocked by my crudeness, and so was I. But I'd reached my breaking point: shitty customers, corporate BS, long hours, working hard despite physical pain again during the most demanding weeks of the retail year. My very first Christmas had been its own ordeal thanks to my injured right shoulder, which required surgery in May 2008 to repair.

"Don't use that language on the floor!" he barked.

"You're kidding, right? That's *all* Phil had to say about my using the stool? Not, 'Hey, it's great that Caitlin is willing to keep working with an injury and help us out through the holidays'?"

No, that was it.

And, for me, that *was* it.

I could still handle, barely, the boredom and low wages, the job's endless folding and sleeving and sizing and schlepping. The replacing of one pile of Third-World-produced overpriced nylon with another almost identical to the last batch. The coworkers with whom, save for a few, I had very little in common.

My body was getting worn out. I'd worked with an injured right shoulder that eventually needed surgery. Then, after a year of pain and stiffness from that injury, my *left* shoulder needed months of physical therapy. Now a broken foot, for no reason the doctor could explain. Working eight hours on my feet also left them throbbing in agony, so tender and sore I could barely walk down my apartment hallway after a shift. I'd lie in bed for two or three hours in such pain I couldn't get to sleep. I didn't want to get into a pattern that might have relieved it—sitting with my feet in ice water after work or gulping down fistfuls of Advil.

What was all this physical discomfort, intellectual stagnation, and emotional abuse in aid of—other than cash? My learning curve had flattened within six months. It was clear no one in senior management took me or my skills or my ambitions seriously. I certainly wasn't doing work that mattered in any larger way, not teaching or medicine or nonprofit or, yes, even journalism. I was wearing out my body and soul to push pricey synthetic materials made for pennies per hour overseas to bored, spoiled suburbanites. And the money was still crap, so lousy that when I asked for a raise Joe told me I'd already gotten one, so small I hadn't even noticed it. Thirty cents an hour.

Now, on top of all that, was this corporate bullshit. The very week I left the folding stool at home, two enormous boxes filled with gift boxes stood piled behind the cash wrap, making that narrow, crowded passageway even more cluttered. When busy, as many as five or six of us were dancing around each other behind the counter, dodging one another. Empty plastic bags scattered there made it easy for us to slip. Empty cardboard boxes cluttered our path to the rear of the store and the fitting room. They also blocked customers' access to, and views of, the watches and knives and gadgets in a display case behind us.

How exactly would my medically necessary stool have posed a hazard?

Like my boss and coworkers, I was trapped in a squeeze play between the huge corporation that considered us interchangeable cogs and too many customers who treated us like morons. I was seriously starting to reconsider the jobs I'd so handily rejected a few years earlier, like babysitting, even cleaning houses. The income would be tax-free, I wouldn't have to stand for hours—and no jerk client earning ten times my wage would dismiss my intelligence because it amused him to do so.

The job had been really enjoyable for a while, then merely enjoyable, then bearable. It was now heading for intolerable. Only the camaraderie of my coworkers had made it worth continuing. The store felt like our own little island, even in the middle of a sterile, soulless mall, our staff a consistent and reliable crew that worked hard, laughed often, and got along well—and sold a ton of merch, even through a recession. We were proud of that. We put up with racist, insulting customers. We trained regularly and knew our products. We passed our "secret shops." We won attaboy letters and complimentary comment cards from customers. One of us—Shaniqua—had even sold an impossible $16,000 worth of product in one shift. *We rocked!*

Intrusions from corporate were something we dreaded and grudgingly tolerated. Those distant, faceless executives paid our checks, but we were bugs on the windshield to them and we knew it. And we didn't like it.

Phil, the perpetually genial district manager, knew my name, and had always greeted me with a smile and interest in how I was doing. His reaction to my folding stool seemed petty, no matter how much I intellectually understood his corporate fear of liability.

Nothing mattered.

From the month we had opened, our store had always been one of the company's top-ranked in sales. From the very start, I'd remained one of the store's most productive salespeople. And our store's stellar sales figures had continued even as the economy plunged into a recession. Nor were we one of the company's larger stores physically. We sold well and our numbers proved it. We all knew, including Phil, who oversaw all our metrics, that our team had played the game well, hard, and consistently.

This was what we got in return?

I originally told Joe I'd be back in the store in late January; my last scheduled day was December 18, as Jose and I were heading back up to Toronto for Christmas. I'd worked up until Christmas Eve the year before.

"I'll have to clear it with HR," he said.

"That's okay. I'll just stop there," I told him. I think he thought I was kidding.

I just wanted out. No more negotiation, no more fruitless hope for improvement.

I told him again the next day that Friday, December 18, 2009, would be my last shift.

"Is it the January scheduling?" he asked. He knew about Jabba the Hutt, the obese, toxic weirdo who had screamed at me in late November; he'd allowed me to go home three hours before my shift's end that night, I had been so upset. But I'd melted down a few times before and never quit.

"No. I just have to go. I'm starting to hate the customers. I'm turning into a bitch. I'm bitter and angry all the time."

"Well, I can see why," he said. "I've pretty much had it with retail myself. I like the pay and the flexibility, but I'm getting sick of it, too." Even his colleague Mike, the easygoing Manhattan store manager who had also initially interviewed me for the job, was about to quit, he said.

"I like my coworkers. I like you guys," I said. "It's the rest of it."

"I hear you. Well, there's an open door if you ever want any hours."

I thanked him.

Word spread quickly through our small team that I was leaving, and I made sure to tell my coworkers as well that I would soon be gone. Most seemed simply disbelieving, as though this were one more of my idle threats or bitter jokes. Who would quit a secure job in the middle of a recession? Didn't I realize how bad things were out there?

I wanted people to know I'd chosen to quit before I simply disappeared from the schedule. I wanted no misunderstandings or idle gossip. I wanted to leave with my head high, with smiles and handshakes and thank-yous. Selfishly, I was curious, too, to see the reactions of the people I'd just spent two years and three months of my life working beside, including three crazy holiday seasons. We'd been in battle together, whether facing a corporate office whose insatiable demands were only getting worse or one more snotty hedge-fund wife. We'd sat through meetings, folded about five thousand T-shirts, picked up about ten thousand dirty, sharp sensor tags—pricking our fingers and sometimes even our feet when they pierced our shoes.

We'd watched our coworkers fall in and out of love, quit, get fired, get pregnant, have babies, dump a live-in girlfriend, add fresh tattoos of a baby's name or a lover to their throat or chest or shoulders. I'd once more managed to deeply offend Peter—who'd lightened up a lot since our first holiday smackdown—just before Christmas 2009 as we thronged behind the crowded counter and I clapped him playfully on one arm,

"Ouch!" he said, piqued. "That's my new tattoo." He made a face, annoyed with me once more.

There were forms of etiquette I still didn't understand with these coworkers and, frankly, probably never would. The world I longed, now, to return to wouldn't focus primarily or exclusively on getting and raising babies or getting a new tattoo or the next pair of shiny new sneakers. I needed—as much as the air in my lungs, by now—to start relying once more upon the shared dreams and middle-class, even bourgeois ambitions of my peers, as psychic fuel. If I stayed much longer at the bottom of the wage scale, surrounded by people who'd given up climbing the ladder, whether for now or for good, I doubted I'd ever get my mojo back.

Now fifty-two, I needed to restake my claim, should there be one, in the professional world where I once had felt most comfortable and, most of the time, still did. I'd gotten an essay published in *Smithsonian's* December 2009 issue, an outlet that's one of journalism's toughest to crack. That boosted my confidence and earned me $1,250 for a few hours' work, wages it took me half a year to earn in the store.

There were a few people I'd miss: Tameisha, Shaniqua, Carl, Jared, Angie, Joe. The rest were good, hardworking people, but the effort of making conversation night after night in an empty store, refolding yet another pile of fleece or polyester, when we really had very little in common—neither our family size, nor neighborhood, nor ambitions, nor even the music we listened to—was wearing thin as well.

"You're leaving! Really?"

Shaniqua, also working extra holiday shifts, was stunned.

"I'll really miss you!" she said, giving me a fierce hug. Even though we'd spent few shifts together, I'd miss her, too. I'd never met someone like her and might not again. I admired her feisty spirit, infectious laugh, and mellow outlook. The woman had four children but had retained the enviably lithe body of a sixteen-year-old, the chic of a Parisienne, and the energy of a toddler. I'd watched her with Jonas, her littlest one, as we sat one afternoon in the stockroom. She seemed a calm, relaxed, happy mother—so very different from the much wealthier older women who stormed into our store, their faces pinched with discontent, desperate to placate their own demanding offspring.

Like almost everyone there, she confided that she, too, was actively searching for a new, better-paying job.

"Hm. Well, at least you tried," said Tameisha in her usual grudging manner, when I told her I'd soon be gone. "You gave it your best shot. You worked hard."

"I enjoyed working with you," said Carl. "Good luck."

In those final few days it felt, suddenly and oddly, as though my former life were crooking its finger at me, beckoning me back. As I frantically rang up another long line of customers, a familiar-looking young man stood before me, a bemused but friendly smile on his face.

"I know you!" I said. I looked at his name on the credit card. It was my financial adviser.

The next day an older woman with brilliant blue eyes and thick white hair came in, looking for a warm coat. She stared at me intently.

"I know you!" she said.

It took us a few minutes to place one another; I used to drop off my antiques on consignment in the shop she then owned.

In all my time at the store, I'd only seen four people I knew socially—two of them in my last few days.

I always wore an old pair of eyeglasses at work, stylish enough that I felt comfortable in them serving upscale customers, but not my best. They were something I could afford to bang up, but they weren't something I could afford to lose.

I didn't realize they had slipped off once more, this time onto the narrow mat behind the counter, where now three to five of us were dodging and weaving wildly as we maneuvered around one another to reach bags and boxes and the two detachers. My spectacles had landed on the floor and someone had stepped on them, snapping them in half.

It felt like another sign from my former life, the one in which I controlled my work space and hours, the one in which people weren't pushing and shoving one another because no one could be bothered fixing a small mechanical problem. I never would have stepped on my glasses at home, nor would anyone in most workplaces. I was fed up with trying to work hard, fast, and well amid such chaos and mess.

Now, my glasses ruined, I saw my exit even more clearly.

* * *

My final day, a Friday, was insane. A blizzard was predicted to drop six to twelve inches of snow the next day. It was also a week before Christmas and shoppers were starting to feel the pressure. I was working eleven a.m. to eight p.m., with thirty minutes for our only break, not the hour we usually got. The pace was ten times faster, and we had almost zero downtime in which to breathe, stretch, chill, or even share a badly needed, tension-busting joke.

We had eight people working, and it still wasn't enough.

At lunchtime, the lines were so long I stood—as we all did—for almost two hours ringing up one sale after another as quickly as possible, barely seconds between transactions. Everyone wanted a gift receipt and a gift box. The receipts didn't pop out half the time, so we'd have to redo the transaction. Getting the boxes, tissue paper, and stickers meant accessing three separate drawers or cabinets, all of which took time and energy. Three of us working all three registers could barely keep pace with the demand. There was no relief. None of us could take the time to pee or sip some water or soda. I had a bad cold and no time to pop an Advil or blow my nose.

In the middle of this, Melissa, our merchandising manager, came in. Her job was to make sure the store looked appealing. What she did, which always drove us nuts, was suddenly—*why?*—move all the stock we'd spent hours, if not days, folding and arranging, to another part of the store entirely. Now we had to refold and rehang much of it. Because, then, it looked so different!

Not.

It wasn't even fresh new stock, just the same stuff we'd been looking at and trying to sell for months now.

No one knew why she did this, other than that it was her job. No one ever bothered to explain to us why this was even necessary. We'd all memorized exactly where the girls' fleeces were and the men's stretch jackets, and the cotton hoodies, and how many of each of them we had. Now it was all changed. In the busiest weeks of the shopping year, this confused already crazed associates; the new seasonal hires barely knew any of our styles or their names, let alone where to find them. Yet we all had to be at the very top of our game. This random re-sorting, with no communication from Melissa or anyone, felt like being kneecapped, typical of The North Face.

When things are fairly busy, it's a pleasure to have a steady stream of buyers and the time flies. But the relentless pressure of the holiday rush is the difference between a trickling creek and Niagara Falls. Despite being, by this point, more than twelve months into the country's worst recession since the 1930s, with gloomy media predictions of a poor holiday season, we were every bit as busy as during the past two years, the store jammed with shoppers happy to drop $150 or $400 or more without qualms. Either people were still running up their credit cards, had retained well-paid, secure jobs, or were so wealthy that the recession was something they only heard about on the nightly news.

Shoppers, many of whom were normally happy to chat or smile, during the holidays were busy, rushed, anxious, tired. So were we. I often didn't smile as I normally would, or make friendly chitchat. By then it took all my reserves of energy to just *keep going* at that breakneck pace; staying calm and civil, attentive and focused.

Of course, for some customers, it wasn't nearly enough.

"Happy holidays," snarled one man sourly as he took his purchase. I'd disappointed him by not being merry and bright.

I'd had it with people's unrealistic and punitive expectations. This wasn't some two-hundred-square-foot privately owned boutique with two racks of exquisite garments, with all the time in the world to sell them, pampering every customer with our rapt and undivided attention. This was a publicly owned national chain store eager for huge profits, in a mall, during the holidays—the busiest and most demanding few weeks of the entire retail year. Yet many customers nonetheless demanded enthusiasm, a sort of robotic automatic pep I found saccharine, insulting, and impossible to achieve at that pace. In normal times, of course, I was happy to smile or converse or just exchange pleasantries. It's what made the job fun.

It wasn't possible during the holidays, whose speed and volume of work and customers demanded every shred of our stamina.

Because I am a perfectionist, this drove me nuts as the odds increased that I might forget something, hand over the wrong change, forget to hand back someone's credit card or remove every last sensor tag.

"Do you have gift boxes?" asked one man. I barely had time to think about my answer when I noticed that a hat in his shopping bag still had a sensor tag on it that I needed to remove. And so, focused on completing that task accurately, I didn't answer within two seconds. So he asked me again.

"I heard you," I snapped.

"Well, you didn't reply."

Technically, he was right. But I could barely handle the job by this point. Too many people wanted too much too fast.

Taking more than even five seconds to consider a thoughtful answer to a question was considered too damn slow. It was as though, once a customer decided we were stupid, we couldn't therefore need any time to reflect or consult a colleague.

In addition to ringing up dozens of transactions within minutes, we also had to answer the phones (five of them in the store) before they rang three times—company policy—which, of course, also looked rude to any customer already standing in front of us.

It's smart to call ahead in the holidays, but this was annoyingly typical:

"Um . . . do you have the jacket? You know, the black one with the belt?"

The phone was now ringing almost nonstop. Every caller expected us to know, and answer immediately from memory, what was in stock, what sizes and colors, and the prices. We carried hundreds of items, about a dozen of which whose prices we did know by heart. But normally we had to put the caller on hold, cross the floor, and check whatever we were being asked for. Sometimes we'd have to write down information from a customer and put an item the customer wanted on hold, but then had no time to take it back to the stockroom and out of the way. So it got thrown behind us onto the long metal credenza, making the place even messier, more crowded and disorganized.

In the midst of all this—thanks to the desperation of competing retailers who had been slashing their prices for months—many customers pushed us hard for a discount or a coupon.

"Isn't *anything* on sale?"

"Everything at the Gap is thirty percent off!"

"I can't believe you're not putting anything on sale."

Their accusations and disappointment fell on our deaf ears. None of these decisions were ours to make, nor those of our manager. Someone, as usual, far away in a corporate office had decided to offer only two or three not-very-popular items at a small markdown. But, as usual, we had to take the brunt of the customers' anger and whining.

I saw Joe only briefly my final day of work in the store; he was in for a few minutes to consult with someone, then gone.

Peter came in for a few hours. He and I had gotten along better since our initial blowup and I was sure he knew I was leaving, but he gave no sign of saying good-bye. As he walked out, pushing through the holiday crowds, I called out a last farewell: "Hey, Peter!"

"Have a good one," he replied blandly, and left.

It turned into the worst day I'd ever seen in our store. If we'd ever needed Joe's guidance, even just his unflappable authority and proven ability to calm our angriest customers, that was it. But he was nowhere around, and it was up to us to figure it out.

As usual, the stockrooms were filled with cardboard boxes, some of which Rob, our terrific, hyperorganized new stock clerk, had neatly labeled and filled. Within a few days they were emptied and piles more had shown up, their contents spilling out haphazardly. If someone wanted a pair of gray fleece men's gloves, size medium, those gloves might be in more than three separate places, if we even had them at all. Knowing our coworkers were being pecked to death by flocks of harried customers out on the floor—like Tippi Hedren in Alfred Hitchcock's horror film *The Birds*—made me want to get in and out of the stockroom as quickly as possible. I'd paw through a few boxes and, if lucky, could quickly find and deliver what a customer wanted. But not always.

That night, justifiably, given how horribly understaffed we were, customers were furious. "You're losing hundreds of sales, you know," snarled one man as he stalked out. "Do you only have one person for the entire sales floor?" asked a woman, not believing any store could be so poorly managed, and leaving hastily when I told her we were, in fact, short staffed that evening.

A middle-aged woman approached me, clearly relieved to have found someone in the chaos whom she felt sure could help her.

"You're the manager, right?" she said hopefully.

"I'm not. But what can I do for you?"

"The service here is terrible! I'm sure you're not like that, but some of the associates are awful."

I knew who she meant—Tameisha, unsmiling and monosyllabic, already overwhelmed by the absurd number of people in the store with only two weary, overworked bodies on the floor and Carl at the cash register to serve them all. It was literally impossible to satisfy everyone, and many of them were getting nasty.

"I know it's crazy in here today," I told her. "There are so few of us here right now to serve the entire store, so I can assure you we're all giving it our very best."

She wasn't the least bit impressed. Nor should she have been. It wasn't her problem the store was severely understaffed. That was a corporate decision: fewer workers = lower labor costs = higher profits.

The loss of who knows how many furious customers swearing never to return? Who cared?

In that brief, predictable, and specific form of madness—the final, frenzied countdown to Christmas Eve—we needed a minimum of three or four associates on the floor at all times in addition to two or three at the registers, not budging from their tasks. Adding three more part-time associates, at even $9 hour apiece for one seven and a half hour shift, would have cost the company barely $200 or so.

While customers expected us to be charming, calm, and welcoming in the appropriate holiday mood, the store expected us—simultaneously—to:

- Answer phones promptly.
- Answer all callers' questions fully and courteously.
- Run to the two stockrooms when needed.
- Carry items from the stockrooms to the floor and back.
- Return all items to the stockroom, while keeping them tidy and organized.
- Unlock the fitting rooms.
- Clear out the fitting rooms.
- Fetch boots and shoes from the stockroom.
- Return all footwear to its proper places in the stockroom so that they wouldn't easily be stolen.
- Keep an eye on potential shoplifters.
- Tidy up the shelves, tables, and racks people were constantly rummaging through.
- Zip up every jacket, and keep them all in size order and hung properly in the right section.
- Restock any areas that started to look thin.
- Clean up—someone had spilled something white and sticky on one of the tables and something yellow and sticky on the credenza. None of us had the time to even grab the Windex and deal with it. An additional one or two stock clerks

doing nothing more than ferrying products out to us, saving the wasted time, energy, and interrupted sales of us running endlessly into the stockrooms, might have saved that evening.

The clock was quickly ticking toward eight p.m. and the end of my final shift. I tried to work up some regrets or sadness, but all I could see were the faces of miserable, angry shoppers wondering why we were so stupid and slow. More than six people were crowded into the short bench in front of the shoe wall, holding out their selections beseechingly like cripples at Lourdes hoping against reasonable hope for the benediction of our attention.

Carl would be there until past eleven p.m., as closing, during the holidays, was at ten p.m., an hour later than usual. Only he and Tameisha—who still faced a ninety-minute train and bus ride home to Manhattan late at night alone—would be left to tidy the store and try to turn the unrelenting mess back into something resembling order.

Carl also had his psychology final exam, a two-hour test, at nine the next morning. No matter what chaos had reigned in the store for the previous shift, no matter how many bodies had stormed through there, Joe—as always—expected to find a clean, tidy, and organized workplace awaiting him when he slid open that heavy glass front door the next morning.

I offered to stay longer, knowing I wouldn't get paid for it, as my labor had been rigidly argued for, and budgeted in, months in advance.

"No, it's okay," Carl assured me, calm as always. "We'll be fine."

And, because they had to, they would.

I pulled off my plastic name tag one last time.

No one asked for it back.

EPILOGUE

I hadn't returned to the mall since the night I quit. I chose a Sunday afternoon, Super Bowl Sunday, February 8, 2010. I went to shop, to be a customer, which felt both liberating and very odd. In the bathroom, I saw a woman I'd served about six weeks earlier. We'd had a long conversation and she had not bought anything. I recognized her immediately; she smiled at me, but clearly didn't remember me. Why would she? If I were her, would I?

I cruised the mall, curious to see how it would feel to be a civilian again. After many long months of frugality, with work finally picking up, I felt confident enough to buy some nonessentials: two cotton pillows at Pottery Barn, two T-shirts at J. Crew, a pair of heels at Steve Madden, some stockings, two cardigans, a pair of costume earrings. I hadn't bought so much, about $400 worth, for months, maybe even a year. I felt disoriented carrying so many shopping bags.

Now the shoe was on the other foot. In most stores, no one acknowledged me—we'd have been dinged on a "secret shop" if we hadn't said hello quickly.

Only one associate seemed happy to chat and be really helpful,

Barbara, a lively, knowledgeable seventy-one-year-old part-timer, a fifteen-year veteran at one of the women's clothing stores—yet another chain that had recently removed all sizes larger than twelve from its racks. I was annoyed by this and told her, suggesting, nicely, she tell corporate—even knowing, by now, what a waste of time it probably was to try to send any message up the ladder to decision makers. I was now a customer, a fussy one midrecession, the kind retailers kept insisting they wanted to woo and win.

I finally entered The North Face, a little nervous, not sure what sort of welcome, if any, might await. I was limping; my left hip had become painfully arthritic in the past few months. I saw Joe and smiled—it took him a minute to recognize me in my dressy outfit.

"Hey!" he said, smiling with pleasure. "Did you have surgery?" He'd already seen me through one operation—my shoulder surgery in May 2008—so it was a good guess. I wasn't there yet, I told him.

We shook hands, exchanged a chaste kiss on the cheek. It felt good to see him again. I missed his easygoing nature and our conversations about everything from family and travel to sports. We started chatting animatedly and he introduced me to a curious young woman at the register: "This is Caitlin. She used to work here."

What he told me only confirmed the wisdom of my decision to quit, and its timing. Every store manager in our district had recently been written up—that is, sanctioned internally—for a variety of petty infractions. Now he, too, was looking for a new job, preferably out of retail entirely. He had just spent two nights in the hospital on an intravenous tube, suffering a severe digestive inflammation.

"I've been a medic. I've been shot at. This is more stressful," he said.

You could practically hear the corporate buzz saw heading toward him. Forget what great sales numbers he and his team—us—had produced for the past two-plus years. Forget his unusual and impressive ability to hire and retain so many of his original staff. Forget the numbers we'd brought in during the worst recession in seventy years. Forget the fact that we'd passed our "secret shops" with flying colors for months at a time.

Like me, Joe was sick of the retail game. It was rigged and bare-knuckled and just not worth it. Whether he stayed or left, no matter our skills or hard work or collegiality or sales, seemed irrelevant to The North Face, whose limber neon-nylon-clad athletes, scaling the Himalayas and fording distant icy rivers, would gaze impassively from their glossy posters no matter who folded the T-shirts or sleeved the jackets below them.

In this army—colonel, customer, or corporal—we were all expendable.

ACKNOWLEDGMENTS

As soon as I started my retail job, several fellow writers were convinced there was a book in it, and as it became reality, their moral and practical support were invaluable: thanks to Salley Shannon, Ulrich Boser, Kim Pittaway, and Sheena Disher, my first readers. *New York Times* writer Ginger Thompson helped me solve one especially thorny problem. Fellow writer and author Scott Bowen offered helpful advice and consistent moral support. Karen Sihra knew well the challenges of moving from low-wage work to high-level intellectual production and helped me weather it. Sally Yardley gave the manuscript a helpful final read.

I was lucky to have two terrific researchers, Peter Holslin and Kelly Ebbels; thanks to colleagues Randy Dotinga and Tim Harper, respectively, for suggesting these two young journalists.

My agent, Kathleen Anderson, is the perfect blend of ferocious and supportive. Thanks to my editor, Courtney Young, for her skills, sensitive eye and patience, to Adrian Zackheim for his enthusiasm, and to Amanda Pritzker, Portfolio's publicist. Production editor Jennifer Tait, copy editor David Cole, art director Joe Perez, and interior designer Amy Hill all gave the book their tremendous skill and attention.

My partner, Jose R. Lopez, was his usual patient and helpful self, from putting up with both our sofas covered in research materials to half-cooked (if at all) meals. A fellow journalist, his insights and criticisms were invaluable.

I spoke to many industry experts and retail veterans, all of whom were generous with their time and insights, including George Whalin, Paco Underhill, Mel Kleiman, Jack Mitchell, Nikki Baird, Deborah Weinswig, Milton Pedraza, Sarah Welch, and Peter Tovell. Thanks also to Christopher DeMeo, Dave Andrews, Kristin Daley, and Keshav Shivdasani of Reflexis, Inc.

Thanks to my *New York Times* editors: Phyllis Messinger for finding me a valuable source, and Phyllis Korkki, who assigned me the "Preoccupations" column in the *Times* that was the germ of this book. Pat Eisemann, a publicist at the *Times*, was a bastion of good cheer and great ideas.

During my time at the store, I visited France, and paid my respects at the Breton grave of my mentor, Philippe Viannay, who founded Journalists in Europe, an eight-month fellowship in Paris that forever changed my ideas about journalism. He believed immersion was essential to understanding a subject; his vision, passion, and compassion were exemplary and inform my work today, twenty-nine years later.

My parents, Ron Kelly and Cynthia von Rhau, both former filmmakers and journalists, were always totally supportive of my retail work, never questioning my commitment to it or wondering why I wasn't "doing better."

My store colleagues had no idea any of this would become a book, and that was never my goal for working there with them, but came much later. I owe them all thanks and gratitude for their patience, help, and friendship—especially to Joe and Angela for taking a chance on me. I wish them all the best.